CHASING BABY

AN INFERTILITY ADVENTURE

Morwenna Trevenen

GREAT PLAINS
PUBLICATIONS

Great Plains Publications
320 Rosedale Avenue
Winnipeg, MB R3L 1L8
www.greatplains.mb.ca

Great Plains Publications gratefully acknowledges the financial support provided for its publishing program by the Government of Canada through the Canada Book Fund; the Canada Council for the Arts; the Province of Manitoba through the Book Publishing Tax Credit and the Book Publisher Marketing Assistance Program; and the Manitoba Arts Council.

Design & Typography by Relish New Brand Experience
Illustrations © Sigrid Ellis
Printed in Canada by Friesens

LIBRARY AND ARCHIVES CANADA CATALOGUING IN PUBLICATION

Title: Chasing baby : an infertility adventure / Morwenna Trevenen.
Names: Trevenen, Morwenna, author.
Identifiers: Canadiana (print) 20220140707 | Canadiana (ebook) 20220140731 | ISBN 9781773370750 (softcover) | ISBN 9781773370767 (ebook)
Subjects: LCSH: Trevenen, Morwenna. | LCSH: Infertility, Female—Patients—Canada—Biography. | LCSH: Infertility, Female—Psychological aspects. | LCGFT: Autobiographies.
Classification: LCC RG201 .T74 2022 | DDC 362.1981/780092—dc23

ENVIRONMENTAL BENEFITS STATEMENT

Great Plains Publications saved the following resources by printing the pages of this book on chlorine free paper made with 100% post-consumer waste.

TREES	WATER	ENERGY	SOLID WASTE	GREENHOUSE GASES
8	670	4	28	3,630
FULLY GROWN	GALLONS	MILLION BTUs	POUNDS	POUNDS

Environmental impact estimates were made using the Environmental Paper Network Paper Calculator 4.0. For more information visit www.papercalculator.org

Canadä

FSC
www.fsc.org
MIX
Paper from responsible sources
FSC® C016245

To Kyle, who knew I was a writer before I did,
and to all of the breeding-challenged folks out there

Contents

Introduction

Do *you have kids?* This seemingly innocuous getting-to-know you question can really sting sometimes. The question itself is understandable, but what comes next is sometimes a doozie: *No kids? Oh, why not?*

Or *Adoption? Why? Why not try the natural way? That's the fun part! The TRYING!* Or the ever popular *Have you tried (insert suggestion that worked for their friend's sister's cousin). Or maybe (insert yet more suggestions)?*

We smile and give our well-worn responses to these questions and suggestions, but it feels a little bit like a knife in the guts every time. Watching our friends and family all around us just having babies, like it's sooooo simple, brings on an odd mix of emotions. On the one hand, we're so happy for them. Truly. It's a wonderful thing to watch people you care about getting what they want out of life. On the other hand, there's that uninvited twinge of jealousy and anger, this inner dialog of *Why does it have to be so hard for us? I don't think I can handle another baby shower. My heart breaks every time you pass me your beautiful, perfect little burrito baby.* Someone tries to hand me their baby to hold, saying that they won't break, and in my head I'm thinking *They won't, but I bloody well might.*

There's also this whole other level of irrational anger at folks who choose to have big families, this idea that anyone who has more than two kids is just being greedy. Share the wealth, people! Or just don't have so many. I have this constant battle inside me between the woman with a strong desire to be a mother myself, the person who fiercely believes in human rights and the right to have any type or size of family that you want, and the environmentalist who believes that seven billion people is just too damned many for this world, so having lots of kids seems just plain irresponsible. It's exhausting inside my head, folks.

I have several friends who also had trouble conceiving. Some of them had been trying for five to ten years, so every time I start to feel like a cynical, miserable old coot, I force myself to remember that I'm not alone. We took great solace in each other and in having people around who knew exactly what we were going through. Then, one by one, they all got pregnant. Hooraaaaayyyyy. This is wonderful news, and they still fully understand the pain of infertility, but it is a little lonely feeling like the only one left who hasn't found a way out of it.

My advice, such as it is, to anyone going through this is to stay strong. Even though you feel really isolated, you are not alone. So many people are experiencing struggles around infertility, the trials of child-rearing, unwanted pregnancies—you name it.

This is why infertility needs to be spoken about more widely. You just never know what kind of hurt is lying just below the surface.

Part

1

The Plan

Do you remember when twenty-five seemed SUPER old? I sure do. I've always been a planner. I'm a list-maker. I can clearly remember being a kid and dreaming about what my life would be (as one does). I didn't do the whole creepy wedding scrapbook or obsess over what my signature would look like if I married Dreamboat McGee, who of course had no idea who I was, but I did have a basic plan. The details of said plan often changed, like what kind of career I would have, what kind of person my partner would be, and what kind of house we would have, but the basic plan was set in stone. By the age of twenty-five I would be married, have a career, a house, a dog, and two kids either already, or on the way. I was always going to be a mom. Obviously!

TO DO:
Graduate university
Get great job (obvs)
Meet perfect partner
Marry said unicorn
Buy house
Acquire dog
Have two children
Travel, live a good life etc.

SPOILER ALERT! That's not the way things panned out. I did graduate university, but the other things remained elusive.

Vivid Dreams

My belly is heavy. My womb is full with her and the goo that protects her from the world. Just in this moment, she is mine and we share this body. I have little conversations with my round fullness and imagine that she can hear. It's our time. Uncomfortable and terrifying but fleeting. And she is mine.

Then she's in my arms, and I think my heart will burst. A mixture of laughter, disbelieving hysteria, and sobbing bubbles up and out of me in a wet mess punctuated with whimpers, sobs, and hiccups. She's here and she is mine. And I am hers. From this day forward.

I can SMELL her. I can FEEL her. Her sweet, fuzzy little head, nuzzled against my chin and neck. I can hear her little coos and feel her wee breaths against my skin, and I melt with them. I can feel the fear and excitement and know that nothing will ever be the same again. Her hands and feet are so tiny.

I know her name.

Then, I wake.

Twenty-Five

I guess I was technically "adulting"—I mean I lived on my own, worked and paid my bills, but HOW DID I EVER THINK I'D HAVE IT ALL FIGURED OUT BY THEN?! I was renting an apartment, trying to make a living in theatre while working several other jobs to pay the bills, finally recognizing my own bisexuality, dating a bunch (sorry mom), and generally had no clue what I was doing with my life. I was managing to feed myself, but cans of tuna, KD, and cheap pizza were my staples, with apples and bananas thrown in because, you know, "healthy living." Maybe I still had some growing up to do, so "The Plan" still existed, it just got pushed back a few years. By thirty, SURELY, I'd have it all figured out. Because thirty was, like, legit adulthood. I was still going to be a mom; I just had to figure out how to properly take care of myself first.

TO DO:
Buy milk
Do laundry
Eat something green
Get some exercise
Pay bills
Start a savings account (yeah, right)
Travel
Marry unicorn, who hopefully has better job prospects than me
House and dog
Babies

I also started a simultaneous plan to get what I wanted from life for my own damn self. #feminism I figured that eventually I would figure out a career path that would be more sustainable, and since my taste in partners was seemingly abysmal, why did I need a partner to have a family anyway? I had the parts, all I needed was the sperm and the ability to support myself and my kids. Oh, what a sweet summer child I was.

When I first met my husband, I disliked him immediately.

I was on tour for a theatre production. The theatre company gave us more money on our meagre actor's paychecks if we didn't take their… er… "lovely" accommodations while touring other cities. I had a three-month block in Calgary, where I stayed with my brother for a couple of weeks before a dear friend offered to let me come and live with her, her boyfriend, and their roommate—Kyle. I had no clue what a gem he was, and though I acknowledged that he was objectively cute and seemingly charming, I had no interest other than friendship. He liked to stay up late, play hockey, drink beer, generally be loud, and leave his dishes to pile up until later. He tracked mud across the floor with his boots. I'd get home after a show, and he would be eating cereal out of a salad bowl using a spatula because they were the only clean dishes in the house. Gross.

He was like complete chaos to my need for order.

Growing up a nerdy outcast, I believed that these types of guys were the enemy, meant to be shunned and avoided. "Other." What I didn't notice at the time is that he is also very intelligent, caring, kind, and funny. His direct approach to pretty much everything is really refreshing, and he can be incredibly thoughtful. Preconceptions aside, he was a fun roommate, and by the end of my three-month stay there I was happy to call him my friend, but ONLY my friend. After all, my unicorn-partner was going to have the following attributes:

Good values (racists, homophobes etc. need not apply)
Hard worker
Great sense of humour
Musical
Loves the arts
Humble
Kind
Considerate lover (sorry again, Mom)
Not a jock, cuz ew sports
Loves dogs

Wants a family
Good cook
Tidy
Handy (Not to be confused with Handsy)

I mean, he may not have every single attribute on the list, but it's a numbers game and MOST of a really demanding list is pretty amazing. For the following five years we remained long-distance friends. He would hit on me, I would say no, and we would go about our separate lives, occasionally cracking wise on Facebook. He dated, I dated, he hit on me, I said no. Repeat. I made some colossally stupid choices in my own dating life and eventually tripped and fell into my career in decorating. Through it all, there was this buddy, Kyle, off in the distance.

Theatre didn't seem like it was going to enable me to provide for a family, and I was spending more time and making more money painting houses than I was on the stage, so I put my big girl pants on, went back to school, and started my career as a decorator, which I thought would pay better and still allow me to be creative. Welp! It turns out that decorating doesn't pay terribly well either, and some of those positive thinking books were enough to convince me to give my head a shake, ditch the douchebag I had been dating, and start over. I was going to find better. I was going to make my life better! I was still going to achieve "The Plan." Somehow.

But then, one of those lovely-yet-wrong relationships having just ended, I had to go to my brother's wedding. Kyle once again asked if we could try a "date" while I was out visiting and, to both of our surprise, I said "Sure! Why not?" Even more of a shock was that we had a wonderful time. WTAF. We ended up with an instant connection that, in spite of ourselves, we were both determined to ignore and write off as simply a fun weekend and nothing more. Back to our separate lives we went because he was SO not the one for me. Pfft. Obviously!

Then Kyle ruined everything. Rude.

He texted me out of the blue about a week after I got home to say that he found himself missing me. And he didn't like it. Not one bit.

We started to talk and text constantly. Then we started to date long distance, but only casually, while still seeing other people. (Insert more poor choices here).

We kept right on missing each other, talking constantly, and the ache of being apart was surprisingly strong. One day we were chatting after work, wishing one of us could hop a plane and fly out to the other. He couldn't come to me because he was in the middle of rehearsals for a show of his own while teaching full-time. I, however, had left my illustrious acting career, almost finished decorating school, and was now working as an in-house decorator at a local boutique.

I quickly called a colleague and she excitedly agreed to take my shifts to support "young love." I booked a ticket on my credit card, tossed random things into a suitcase, got a ride to the airport, called my parents on the way to let them know I was leaving town, and within three hours I was in his arms. *Me! The planner! The non-impulsive one.* Good lord, what had this man done to me?

For the next several months we went back and forth visiting when we could, and we filled in the blanks as best we could with texts, emails, phone calls, short videos, communication apps—basically anything technology had to offer. But after about six months of long distance, we decided that it just wasn't working. It was just too hard.

So, he decided to move across the country to be with me. HOLY CRAP.

It could have gone so, so badly, but it didn't. We fell madly, barf-inducingly in love! We made forts for movie marathons, enjoyed camping and nerding out over the same books and TV shows, and generally were blissfully happy. This guy, that I had totally misjudged, was nothing like I had thought. While not a musician, he loves music. He loves the arts, teaches drama, loves being outdoors, loves dogs, is thoughtful, funny, and creative. He's not so much a fan of cooking, but beggars can't be choosers. He taught me to like and understand hockey (I'm a REAL Canadian now!) and he even had a similar life plan! Gold star!

He got a job in our school division, joined a local hockey team, and started making friends, and I decided to combine all of my talents and education into what would hopefully make sense to support a family—real estate. I had the decorating and painting background, this would surely make me a better living than acting or decorating, and the ability to work from home during the day, theoretically with kids, with Kyle taking over as parent in the evenings while I went off to show properties, sure seemed like a good plan. I didn't even have any idea, at the time, just how much I would use my theatre degree! What could possibly go wrong? "The Plan"—here we come!

We got married in 2013, just over two years after he moved. It was like a fairy tale—literally, he had a sword by his side at the wedding and everything—and we were ready for the happily ever after part.

Ri...right?

The Start of Our Infertility Journey

Well, I'd found my partner (good for me!), and we both wanted a family. We were excited to have kids and to stumble through the adventure of parenthood together, but we wanted to enjoy a few months of newlywed life before getting down to business. We continued to grow, and love, and laugh, (and get irritated at each other's idiosyncrasies while we shared a small house. It can't all be hearts and flowers, people.) and we decided that I should stop taking birth control and start trying to get pregnant on our upcoming trip.

After about six months of official marriage, we went on our honeymoon to Florida to play in Harry Potter World. (see: nerd romance). While we were there, we discovered two big things:

1. a place called "Total Wine." This is a literal warehouse of ridiculously cheap alcohol. Seriously, this was like finding Santa's workshop, but for adults. Why doesn't Canada have this? I mean, it's probably good that we don't, for our own good, but still. It was a sight to behold.

2. what it felt like to be excited, happy, and terrified all at once. We started "trying" to get pregnant. Which, at the beginning, is more about not *preventing* pregnancy, and actually is a lot of fun. Several times during that week, as we went about our family visits, Universal studio rides, beach days etc. we grinned at each other and whispered, "did we just make a baby?" (Not amidst the family visits and public rides, of course. That would be gross. We're

not animals!) It was like we had this enormous secret, and we couldn't wait to tell our friends and family when we were pregnant! We even planned ridiculous (and, of course, hilarious…possibly with puppets) ways to tell everyone. The cryptic picture with a Facebook post, a large and theatrical spitting out of wine at a family function, followed by a "Right! I can't have that! It's not good for the BABY!" which was undoubtedly going to be followed by squeeeees and hugs and jumping up and down etc. So, you know, our feet were firmly planted on the ground and we were completely rational.

It hadn't really occurred to either of us that infertility might be a problem for us. Yet as the months stretched into a year with no pregnancy in sight, we started to realize that things weren't going to be so easy for us. I guess I figured that my uterus was perfectly happy just sitting around and waiting to be taken out on a test drive. In actuality, maybe it wasn't such a fan of the many, many years on and off of birth control. Maybe it retired? Maybe it decided to go on strike in protest? Who knows. We read the books and blogs, and we took many, MANY types of advice from friends, family, and strangers on how to get me knocked up.

What felt like eons passed. We tried the constant temperature taking, the date counting and timing, the weird, post-coital yoga positions that are supposed to help, different underwear for Kyle, certain foods to try. And, lemme tell you, the "trying" was getting less and less fun. Sex is a wonderful thing, especially with someone you love. Sucking all of the fun out of it with temperatures, timing, the fact that it HAS to happen, and the insane pressure of thinking that maybe *this* will be THE TIME doesn't exactly get you in the mood.

I was also not drinking alcohol, taking prenatal vitamins, avoiding sushi and green tea and soft cheeses, and had SWITCHED TO DECAF COFFEE on the odd chance that I was pregnant. It may have been overkill at the time, but I was determined to do this right. I would like my hero biscuit, please. The point is, after one-and-a-half years of agony over trying and failing to get pregnant, we decided to go to plan B.

Well, plan B was actually multiple visits to multiple doctors, fertility treatments, hormones, and fabulously invasive tests to figure out what the problem was. I got my first (but not my last) taste of what it feels like to be treated like a nameless, faceless number—a cog in the endless infertility machine.

After spending about five minutes with a fertility specialist, I was handed a prescription for hormones. This without any test to see what my hormone levels were and despite the fact that TWO doctors had made comments about me probably having a hormone imbalance based on my monthly fluctuations of weight, emotions, general PMS symptoms etc. The specialist gave me an internal ultrasound and then sent me home with a prescription for Letrozole to presumably get me pregnant. He sent me for an HSG test to make sure my, er, parts work (and they do, thank you very much) but nothing in the way of blood tests etc.

I also tried acupuncture three times a week, and—literally—hundreds of pills per day of herbs prescribed by my acupuncturist/doctor. Interesting experience. SO much money and time and super gross teas.

Super.

Gross.

The good news was that we were both healthy and our infertility was unexplained. So…yay? Or would it have been better to know what was wrong and see if it could be fixed? The bad news was, I am apparently REALLY sensitive to hormone manipulation. I wasn't even on one of the crazy ones that feels like it would come with a reality show contract at the end. I was supposedly on one of the "less offensive" hormones.

Kyle never really knew what he was going to come home to. For the first six to seven months that I was on the fertility hormones, I was completely irrational. Letrozole was a disaster for me. I was either sobbing in a mess on the floor over nothing, or completely, inexplicably, full of rage. All of the gym combat classes in the world couldn't take the edge off of my anger. The benefit of this was that my physical fitness had never been so high-level; endless push-ups (even one-armed ones) didn't faze me, and I've never been the most athletic gal around by any stretch—so, yay for extra testosterone! All of this, plus the brutal emotional pain every month for almost two-and-a-half years of getting hopeful and excited, thinking that FINALLY I was pregnant, only to get my period less than an hour after taking a pregnancy test, was enough.

We decided that this was no way to live. We had always planned to have one child naturally and adopt another one. Kyle was adopted and has always wanted to give a child the same love and opportunity that he was given. Kids need love, opportunities, patience, those flashy wheelie shoes (apparently), and a crapload of other stuff, both tangible and otherwise. People who would truly love to be parents need a kid to love and give all of said things to. I adore this idea, so we decided to skip straight ahead to Plan C. Adoption.

Part
2

Adoption

U pon going to explore the adoption possibility and process, we certainly discovered some things, both about ourselves, and the process. In Canada adoption is provincially regulated, so what happens in one province is not the same as in another. In my home province of Manitoba, adoption is not subsidized by the government. The legal fees, adoption fees, salaries for the social workers who run the adoption agencies, hotel fees, travel fees if bio-mom is from a rural area (or if you are), processing fees, criminal record check fees, fingerprinting fees, doctor's note fees, just because fees, extra fees, kick-you-in-the-teeth fees, and unexpected surprise fees are all paid by the adoptive parents to the tune of about $12,000-$20,000 on average. This is just for local adoptions. International adoptions are between $30,000-$40,000 and have another whole (and years-long) process, and Child and Family Services (CFS) adoptions are another ball of wax altogether.

We also learned that most adoptions in our province are mandatorily open. You jump through hoops, fill out endless file applications, compile two pages of pictures that show who you are as best they can, and a cover letter, spend a bunch of money, get checked out by the government and a doctor, and then wait. If a birth mother chooses your file and wants to meet you, and then that meeting goes well, and then the baby gets placed with you, and in twenty-one days the biological parents don't change their minds, TADA! You are now a parent! Easy peasy.

Warning: "the call" could happen with a few months' notice, a weeks' notice, or twenty-four hours' notice. (EEP!)

They say not to prepare. Don't read the books, don't buy the things, or prepare the nursery. It could be too painful if you're not chosen, or if it takes years to be chosen. Live your life and wait, which makes sense

in theory. It doesn't work so much in practice. In other words: "Don't freak out." (Spoiler alert: we freaked the fuck out).

In the meantime, we filled out application after application. They were long and exhausting to fill out but asked some important questions. Things like how you will discipline your child, how you will handle things like bullying, sexual orientation and gender identity, different cultures etc. How do you and your partner discuss and/or fight over difficult situations? Will you use daycare? Etc. etc. etc. There are SO many good questions and important things to consider for any prospective parent.

There are also a ton of checkbox questions that aren't checkbox types of questions. How many drinks, cigarettes, drugs are you comfortable with the mother consuming while pregnant? During which point of the pregnancy are you comfortable with how many drinks or drugs consumed? How much of which ethnicities are you comfortable with (percentage-wise)? Which genetic disorders are you comfortable with? Are you comfortable with either bio-parent having a criminal record? Questions like these are almost impossible to answer—especially in a "pick a box to check" kind of manner! They tell you to be honest, both with them and with yourselves, but it's uncomfortable, and we felt like horrible people for ruling out certain things.

But then there are questions like "How will your lives change once you become a parent" with only about an inch of paper space to answer! In the end we chose "In every imaginable way" as our answer and hoped for the best, thankful that they couldn't see our furrowed brows and sarcastic expressions on the page.

Next you get to do home studies. These are a trip. We did five of them, and surprisingly only one was actually in our home. These are like friendly interrogations with a social worker, but without the bare lightbulb swinging from the ceiling. They really want to get to know you in great detail. They want to know all about every traumatizing thing that has ever happened to you and how you dealt with it. They even want to know about your sex life, which isn't at all SUPER AWKWARD, especially when trying your best to look like a good, wholesome potential parent. "How often are you two intimate? How many times a week? Do you feel satisfied and emotionally connected in your sex life?"

In one of our home studies, our social worker asked us what we would do if our new baby either reacted badly to, or turned out to be allergic to, our dog. Charlie is the best dog in the world. I know everyone says that, but we truly mean it. She's half Husky, and half (maybe) Rottweiler and German Shepherd, and a complete suck. She is my constant companion, and I can't even put into words how she has enriched our lives. She sheds nonstop, which is a pain to keep up with, but she also ADORES children and is endlessly patient with them. She spent her first few years as my stepbrother's dog with my baby niece as she grew into a toddler. My niece would cruise around the coffee table as she learned to walk, stepping right over and across Charlie, who would barely raise an eyebrow. This dog will drag me over to kids when we see them if we're out for a walk because she just wants to lick their faces and love and protect them forever. It's beautiful and heartbreaking for me, and probably terrifying for the small children who don't know that she won't hurt them! She loves to camp, run, play, get belly rubs and sleep at your feet. She's terribly afraid of thunderstorms, and there have been many moments when she has truly saved the day for us. If I'm having a sad moment or a bad day, she comes running to comfort me. She's part of our family, and we will be devastated when she eventually dies, which isn't allowed to happen for a long, LONG time—if the universe is listening...ahem.

Okay, I guess that's a lot of gushing about a dog, but hopefully it helps illustrate how big of a role she plays in our lives.

When our social worker asked us this question, we shot each other a quick look, and gave the "correct" answer. Real baby trumps fur baby, of course. There's no danger of Charlie not being good with a kid, but if he reacts poorly to her, or is allergic, of course we'd find another home for her. It would be incredibly, brutally hard, but you do what you have to do, of course.

After a two- three-hour appointment with the social worker (who was very nice, by the way) just sitting around and talking, we were completely exhausted. Being physically and emotionally drained is just something we got used to throughout this process. But, again, if we get to be parents at the end of it—all of this would be well worth it.

We couldn't help but wonder how different things would be if all parents had to go through something like this. Not as intense, perhaps, but even just a weekend seminar or something to plant the seeds in parents' minds about how they are going to navigate their way through life with a kid; come up with some sort of a plan on how to handle situations as they arise, or even how they, as a couple, will keep their relationship strong when figuring out how to do one of the hardest jobs on the planet.

Childhood Christmas

There are gifts sparkling under the tree, with twinkly lights and tinsel glinting. Tinsel that always, ALWAYS would rather attach itself to a nearby sweater than the branch we had draped it over…and must be kept high enough that our dog can't get at it, or else tomorrow's walk will suck.

As usual on Christmas Eve, we are at church. Sheesh, our Anglican reverend is a fan of loooong sermons, and even longer services. They are so boring for us kids, but at least the music is pretty, and there's something so comforting about hearing the nativity story again. Maybe it's the tradition and familiarity of it. The carols and chants are mesmerizing and soothing, even though I have to stay in my seat this time. Both of my parents are in the choir, so sometimes when the children's time is finished, I simply march right up to the choir loft and snuggle in next to my dad. I'm probably getting too old for that, now, but it helps pass the time during the two-and-a-half-hour service. He quietly keeps me entertained by teaching me to read music in hymn books under his breath, while the Reverend drones on about…something. Even though I should stay in my seat this time, at least the Christmas service is special. And I have to be EXTRA good: SANTA is coming tonight! Be good, Wenna. Don't fidget. Don't even think bratty thoughts.

My new dress is pretty, if uncomfortable. Why is it so scratchy? And the elastics around my arms are too tight. Don't fidget. Does that count as a complain-y thought? Will Santa know?! Oh well. Soon we will go home and maybe sing carols around the piano (no, I'm not making this up), or watch a Christmas movie before bed.

We'll have to put out cookies and milk for Santa and a carrot for Rudolph. Then William and I each get to choose one present from under the tree. ONE. Which one will I choose?! I'll have to carefully shake them to make sure they're not clothes or something boring. Maybe my big brother will let me sneak into his room again. He's always nicer to me at Christmas. Then I'll have to try to get some sleep, but I'll probably be up half of the night, listening for Santa…and STARING at that present. You see, the presents we got to choose are for first thing in the morning, so that when Will and I wake up obscenely early, we can amuse ourselves with our one present until we are allowed to wake up mom and dad at 7 a.m. But, I mean, since they will both take FOREVER getting out of bed, and going through the bathroom, and going downstairs to turn on the tree etc., we will help out by waking them up at 6:55 instead. To make sure we're on time and downstairs for 7. We're so clever. It never works, though.

Cut to me, mom, and William, sitting on the landing:

"Daddy. Daaaaaaad! Hurry UP!"

"I'm coming! Take it easy."

"What's taking so long? Pee FASTER!"

"John, the kids are inching down the stairs…"

"Just wait! I'm coming, and I have to go downstairs first to make sure Santa didn't have any trouble."

….

"But then presents?"

"First coffee. Then stockings. Then you have to EAT SOMETHING. Then presents."

"UUUUUUUUUGGGGHHHHHH. Fine."

Luckily, my mom is a smarty-pants. She makes these special muffins at Christmas. They are packed with all of the things— nuts, apples, carrots, raisins, eggs, coconut, whole wheat. One of these dense little hockey pucks, and you're GOOD! Onward to presents! We'll snack later and then head over to Grandma and Grandpa's for dinner, and I can show my cousin my new toys. I love Christmas so much, and I'm so excited to pass along these traditions to my own kids when I grow up.

T-Rex

A t this point in our "hurry up and wait" scenario, we felt like life had been put on pause. The thoughts, anxiety, and preparation for a baby to (hopefully) arrive any day became all-encompassing. While we waited for our "real" life to begin, we tried to enjoy the moment. We lived to the fullest as much as we could, particularly doing things that we knew would be more difficult with kids—travel, sleeping late, going out for dinners on short notice. It was our time, so we tried to soak it up.

We also knew that we needed to embrace the ridiculousness in our lives to distract ourselves from our pain.

Now, Kyle isn't so much a fan of getting me "conventional" presents, as he prefers to get me something that I would never buy for myself but might get a kick out of. Sometimes it's a swing and a miss, but sometimes it's amazing. For my thirty-fifth birthday, he decided that I needed one of those inflatable T-Rex suits. Because of course I do.

At first I thought "Oh great, yet another thing that will take up space in our home that I won't use." Then I tried it on. Guys. GUYS! I'm like freaking Chewbacca-Mom in this thing! I can't stop giggling! So far, I have walked the dog in it (yes, my neighbours may think I'm a little nuts, but they got to watch me get taken out by a low-hanging branch, so it's a win-win). I watched some *Game of Thrones* with Kyle and the dog, presented pumpkin pies for Thanksgiving, took it to the office to show off Dino-Realtor, I have used it to market some of my property listings, I wore it to a social and a party, and decorated the Christmas tree in it (the picture of this HAD to go on our Christmas cards, obviously).

I have also taken it travelling. Yes, it does require more luggage. Yes, that does cost extra, and yes, we do get incredible withering looks from

some people, but can you really put a cost on ridiculous? (The answer is yes. Yes, you can. We just haven't gotten to that point yet.)

We have taken it to New Brunswick for a family Easter-egg roll, where it sorta died and I had to get some help to hotwire it because the wires that connect the fan/pump to the battery packs weren't working. Yup, you read that correctly. The hotwired suit did spark occasionally, with me inside of it. It worked and it was hilarious, but the whole time I was inside this nylon, *flammable* suit with sparks inside, I was wondering if this was how I was going to die.

We retired suit #1.

We bought another one.

We took it to Kauai for Christmas. If you haven't been to Kauai, there are a ton of adventurous things to do on and around the island: Zip-lines, snorkelling and scuba diving, a five-hour Navy Seal raft adventure that feels like you're hanging onto a galloping horse on water.

I didn't take the T-Rex suit on the raft adventure because, let's face it, that's an incredibly stupid idea and even if it **HAD** been allowed (which

I'm sure it wouldn't have been), I couldn't help but think "Now, *this* is how I die. Drowning or being eaten by some SUPER confused sharks after being blown overboard in an inflatable dinosaur suit. My family will be so proud." I didn't take it on the zip-line either, basically for the same common-sense type reasons. Plus, how the hell would the harness have fit? The zipline folks said it probably would've worked, but I didn't want to test it.

What "Dino-Mo" DID get to do was run around on golf courses, freak out some local chickens (they're everywhere there. For real.), make some tourists' day, and recreate some moments from *Jurassic Park*. We had to... well... kinda, sorta, ...okay I hopped a fence and trespassed onto the field where the Gallimimus run in the first movie. It was only for a moment; the cows weren't freaked out at all, and it was hilarious!

We also took the suit to the top of an incredible mountain range and took silly videos of me in the suit on the cliff. The wind was strong, and for a moment I was certain that, in fact, THIS was how I would die—being blown off of a mountain in Kauai in a giant sail, AKA dino-suit. I did not die, and it was also hilarious. I count that as a win!

On our way home from that trip, our luggage got lost, and we got stranded in Calgary for three days, in -40 degrees, with no luggage or T-Rex suit to help make us giggle. BUT! We have absolutely wonderful friends in Calgary. One of them picked us up and entertained us for the night before letting us crash HARD. He also works with a medical cannabis company, so had lots of extra clothing from trade shows to loan us. So Kyle ran around snowy Calgary in sandals, with cannabis-themed socks, t-shirt, boxers and sweater. I got to run around Calgary in cannabis-themed socks, t-shirt, sweater, and what can only be described as 'MURICA tights—one leg was stars and the other stripes. Yup. We looked amazing and got some hilarious looks. I was so glad that I wasn't in a city where people know me.

We've also taken Dino-Mo to Scotland and Ireland. Ridiculous, inconvenient, expensive, worth it.

The thing is that life tends not to go as planned. Sometimes that's really sad. But we should never underestimate the power of a ridiculous suit, or the ability to laugh at ourselves. Sometimes it's the only way to sanity—even when it seems absolutely bonkers.

Don't Freak Out

After our paperwork was all filled out, boxes checked and questions answered to the best of our ability, our file was completed and approved. Kyle input the phone number for the adoption agency into his phone under the name "DON'T FREAK OUT." We figured that the next time they called us, it would be "the call" and our first instinct would be to lose our shit, so this seemed like a funny and useful idea.

We went about our lives; working, spending time with family, and trying not to think too much and just go with the flow (some days more successfully than others). We'd heard that it could take years to get chosen, so we were trying not to get our hopes up too much just yet. One summer afternoon in 2016, only about two-three months after our file was completed, we spent the afternoon in the park with my brother and niece. Then Kyle's phone rang, with the caller listed as "DON'T FREAK OUT." We tried not to, but if I'm being honest, there were some mild breathing issues as we answered the phone.

A birth mother had chosen us out of twenty-three files that she'd been shown. She wanted us to adopt her beautiful seven-month-old son. We couldn't help but freak out a little. Or a lot. Yup, a lot. We felt ALL OF THE EMOTIONS: ultimate happiness, excitement, sheer terror at the thought of being parents within DAYS, worry at the number of things we needed to acquire and get done to our house, and even more worrying over the fact that we were over $3,000 short, since we hadn't thought we'd get chosen so quickly.

We also felt nothing at all. This is shock. I've experienced it before, but it never stops being weird and disconcerting. We were sort of numb on autopilot, unable to absorb basic information. It didn't matter though; we were going to be parents!

Holy shit.
HOLY SHIT.

My husband is a teacher. I am a real estate agent and I run my business from home. Truthfully, 2016 had been less than kind to us, with one thing after another going wrong with work, expensive repairs in our home, family losses, and me experiencing what seems like the worst financial year on record since starting this new career. We were ecstatic and determined to figure it out; it is just unfortunate that we happened to get the call that we were going to be parents at a time when we had never been more strapped for cash, especially since this particular adoption would cost us $10k over the $3k that we were already short. This was stressful to say the least, and as we plunged ahead into this adventure, we discovered that ours was not going to be the easiest or most straightforward of adoptions. But we were determined to be ready.

The adoption agency had told us that we shouldn't tell too many people our news until everything was finalized. Partly because there are confidentiality clauses to protect the identities of both of us as well as the birth parents. But the rule also existed to protect us emotionally. If you get the chance to adopt, and you tell everyone, put adorable posts on social media, and scream it from the rooftops, and then things don't end up working out, then you've got to tell EVERYONE that sad news after the fact. This could compound your pain and also multiply the dreaded sympathetic head-tilts that you will receive. So then the Facebook posts would be, what? "Just kidding!" "False alarm, lol!" #soclose #almostparents No, thanks.

But this secrecy created some confusion in our social circles when we suddenly couldn't talk, think, or do anything anymore. Though we'd told some of our closest friends and family what was going on so that we could get help acquiring things like toys, strollers, play pens, and general knowledge and so we could organize work (this was two weeks before school started, so right about the time when teachers are working like mad to prepare, AND I had a ton of clients who needed lots of attention from me), our other friends and family members were completely unaware of our new upside-down life. They'd text or call to invite us to things, ask for coffee dates or call to catch up, and we would either pretend everything was fine and we were just busy—though we couldn't say what we had planned for that night, the one after that, or the one after that. So we would end up just being cryptic and sounding aloof, or we'd just plain forget to respond to them, which is also not the best. Here's a little tip: it's WAAAAAAY easier to lie via text message than it is in person or over the phone; especially if you're bad at it and out of practice. Some of the wonderful people in my life must have thought I was just suddenly so weird or going through an early mid-life crisis of some sort.

The agency also told us not to buy anything or prepare a nursery before getting the call. We, more than anyone, understood the pain and sadness that can go along with being surrounded by baby stuff and wondering if we'd ever get the chance to have a baby of our own. Over the years we had become experts at avoiding those aisles in supermarkets, department stores, and stores like Ikea. It had become a simple matter of self-preservation. I hadn't noticed it at the time, but I had become some sort of shopping ninja without realizing it. I knew exactly where to avert

my gaze and which direction NOT to go when out running errands. We figured that since newborns don't really need much more than a bassinet, formula or breast milk, and diapers there would theoretically be time to get everything we needed anyway. But then we were suddenly handed a seven-month-old. They are no longer just eating, sleeping, pooping, and crying burritos. They are sitting up, getting ready to crawl, and needing entertainment and some sort of play area (or, as Kyle lovingly calls it—a baby dungeon). Having a community of friends and family for support was invaluable to help us get our house in order, and subsequently complete *disorder* by filling it up with stuff! We were so proud of ourselves when we spent two days tearing our tiny house apart and cleaning it, purging things we could stand to get rid of. We called those junk picker-uppers and spent hundreds of dollars to have them haul away so much stuff that we probably could've done pretty well at a garage sale if we'd had more time. We had only a few days until we were going to have a baby living with us, people! No time. NO TIME!!! Do you want a crazy, hummingbird version of me? Because this is how we get a crazy, hummingbird version of me.

We then got so much help and so many donations from people that it promptly took up all of the space, and then some more, of all of the things we had just gotten rid of. Our house had never felt so small. It was wonderful at the same time as horrible for a neat freak like me. Come to think of it, this might explain why there was truly such an elated look on the faces of my friends and family who donated so many things to us. Yes, they were helping us big-time, but they were also GETTING THIS CRAP THE HELL OUT OF THEIR HOUSES. Well played, friends. Well played.

In addition to setting up a space for this tiny human, we were also freaking out about what the heck to do with him. Not only did we speed-read a couple of books on what babies this age would need in terms of sleep, food, entertainment/development, we also Googled all things baby. We called all of our doctor friends, psychologist friends, parent friends…pretty much anyone who's ever had contact with a baby. We got conflicting advice, but it felt WAY better than the general "DUH" feeling that coincided with utter terror. We had signed up for this, we had wanted it for ages, and were supposed to be able adults. How had I taken it for granted for so long that I'd simply have a baby without feeling like a panicked moron? Did I expect to just be magically imbued with baby knowledge?

So basically, we didn't tell many people, but having a small sphere of people around us who DID know, who could be excited with us, support us, and just generally know what was going on in our lives, was incredibly helpful. This crazy train is a hell of a ride, so having support that isn't solely from your partner makes sense, or at least it did for us.

What to Wear?

After "the call" and our two-day, Tasmanian Devil-style rampage through our house to make it more baby ready, we had an appointment to meet the birth mother. She had seen our file, and we had seen hers. The files that are available for us to read were pretty basic, though even if they had been as rife with details as if written by George R.R. Martin himself, there was absolutely no way to prepare for this meeting. Again, with ALL of the emotions.

This is the most important job interview I have ever been to.

Ahem. "Hi, my name is Morwenna, and I have always wanted the job of being a mother. I think I'd be really good at it, and I'm willing to work really hard to be the best that I can. My interests include building forts, eating (mostly) healthy foods, and hosting random kitchen dance parties/singalongs. Why, no! Extensive overtime and life changes don't terrify me at all! Please hire me?"

What does one even wear to meet the mother of their potential child? What says, "Please give me your baby"? Should I look modest? Like a schoolmarm or typical storybook mother with a sweater set and pearls? Or funky, fun, and interesting? Is this too low-cut? This too short? Should I have bought mom jeans? I should have bought mom jeans.

What says that this child will be endlessly loved, competently cared for, and will have loads of fun and giggles along the way? How do I show the amazing community of family and friends that surrounds us, and would make the village that would raise this child? Perhaps a slightly creepy t-shirt with pictures of all of them... In the end, I went dressed as myself in a cotton tank top and a floral skirt given to me by a friend.

On top of the general feelings of shock, excitement and terror, a distinct urge to puke and/or poop my pants was added to the mix. As we were sitting in the waiting room full of loving sayings stencilled on the walls, I was saying quietly to myself "I'm not going to barf. I'm not going to barf. … I might barf." It did occur to me that maybe barfing on the birth mother when meeting her for the first time wasn't the best idea. My mom texted to see how we were doing, and I mentioned the frantic battle raging in my tummy, and my fear that I might puke on the birth mother as a thank you for choosing us. Her response was "Well, that would certainly make an impression!" I didn't barf. I did fart a bit though. Kyle made a show of reacting to it, to the point where he even got up and started fanning the door open and closed while giggling and doing impressions of what the meeting could play out like, with the birth mom and social worker walking into a room full of some sort of fart fog, like Pigpen from Peanuts cartoons. But I ask you, what was I supposed

to do? Holding it all in until I exploded one way or another seemed like a worse plan. How odd that THESE are the things I remember!

Kyle was vibrating too, but still managed to be supportive of his mess of a wife. God bless that man. He reminded me that I was once a trained actor, and I could do this. Good point.

What we did to lighten the mood was play games like "I spy." It sounds silly, but it really did help to ease the tension and provide distraction for us both. It even calmed my tummy down a teeny bit…or at least enough to pretend to get control of myself.

Finally, in walked the birth mother who had chosen to meet us. She was sweet, quiet, young, and seemingly nervous too. Obviously, she was nervous! I can't even imagine what she must have been feeling. The whole situation was REALLY AWKWARD. The small talk was unreal. Kudos to our social worker from the adoption agency! This lady is amazing. She was fully aware and sensitive to the fact that we were all brutally nervous, and she did a great job of asking us all questions to try to help the conversation and cut the tension a bit. I suppose the folks who work there see these situations all the time, so they are able to act like complete pros while the rest of us flounder in an emotional ocean.

Kyle had read in the birth mother's file that she was into Anime, so he zeroed in on that to try to start a conversation. It helped a bit but didn't do much to take away the feeling that she was so young, and we, by comparison, felt impossibly old. The great leveller was that we were all terrified. I don't know how long this meeting lasted, but it felt both incredibly short and painfully long at the same time.

After the initial meeting, Kyle and I went for a walk and a coffee to discuss whether or not we wanted to move forward. The social workers suggested that we take an hour or two to discuss things, just the two of us, and then come back to discuss any concerns. They wanted to make sure that we were certain about moving forward before letting us see the baby.

This is when we found out that there were even more, and more, and MORE added costs coming up for us: travel fees, hotel fees because the apartment she was put up in here in town had bedbugs, and more legal fees because the bio-dad refused to be served with the notice of adoption. He had said to "give him up for adoption" when he was informed that she was pregnant, and then virtually disappeared. Because he wouldn't accept this form, our lawyer had to go to court to ask a judge for a waiver

of bio-dad's parental rights, allowing the birth mom to sign adoption forms on her own. This should've been easy, though every time they went to court it cost another $1500-$2000.

The birth mom's home life was a main concern from the beginning, both for us and for the social workers. She had agonized over what to do and had finally decided that adoption was the best decision for all concerned. Brave girl. Amazing girl. She loved her baby and wanted the absolute best for him, which is why she wanted to find a good home for him: to give him opportunities that she felt she couldn't provide. It would also give her the opportunity for a life of her own.

Despite all of this, we really wanted to move forward and meet our potential son. What if this was our only chance to be parents? What if we never conceived on our own or got chosen for adoption again? What if we did, and the birth mom isn't as great as this one? In this case, she was sweet, kind, and someone that we were comfortable having in our lives forever. Plus, she didn't drink, smoke, or do drugs during the pregnancy! That's huge. HUGE.

All of this discussion about our potential baby boy—and we hadn't even met him yet. It makes sense. It protected us, baby, and the birth mom from the experience of attachment and then heartbreak.

Kyle and I were in a big conference room, and the birth mom and baby were with social workers down the hall, filling out paperwork to present to the judge to ask for the waiver. We were waiting to meet this child; barely breathing. And I had to pee. Let's not forget the coffees I had while on our "discussion walk"; my bladder sure wasn't letting me forget! I held it for as long as I could, folks, but it was taking FOREVER, and I really had to go. I snuck out into the hallway to find the bathroom and announced my presence, but no one heard me. I saw the baby boy from the back as he was playing on his tummy on the floor, and my heart leapt up into my throat like in an old cartoon.

After playing "Rock, paper, scissors" to see who would get to hold him first (Kyle won, btw) we were called to come to the meeting room where the birth mom and our social worker were waiting. We chatted a bit more, discussed changing his name and keeping his current name as a middle name, and agreed. Then they brought him in.

At this point I had pretty much been in tears all day, and my stomach had been in knots for days with worry about ALL OF THE THINGS: learning to parent on the fly, getting the house ready, where the F$*# we were going to come up with the money, how work would happen for me, trying not to barf…it all melted away when he appeared in Kyle's arms. I dissolved into tears, yet again. Then Kyle handed him to me. He was beautiful.

Most of that "meeting" is a blur to me now, but I can remember trying to decide how to act. If I was comfortable and loving with him would that make the birth mom feel crappy? But I didn't want to seem stand-offish, either, for fear of appearing like a cold person. Trying to say the right things and be considerate of birth-mom while still enjoying the moment with this beautiful little boy was tricky. Yet holding him was an amazing feeling. I felt like an elastic band that's been stretched too far, or like butter spread over too much bread, yet completely calm at the same time. It's incredibly surreal to consider the possibility that your dreams could be coming true at this exact moment. I don't have the words to describe it.

The Roller Coaster

We had filled out the forms, endured the home studies, signed all the paperwork, paid all the fees, but our adoption wasn't official quite yet. Birth parents have twenty-one days to change their minds and reverse the adoption. Most reversals happen shortly after the baby is born, in the two days that the mom spends alone with her infant in the hospital.

From there, if the two days pass and the birth mom is still on board for placement, then the baby goes home with the adoptive parents and the twenty-one-day countdown begins. These have to be the longest twenty-one days EVER for all concerned.

In cases like ours, where the baby had already been born, the adoptive parents have to spend one "quality visit" with the baby for every month that the baby has been alive before the twenty-one-day period begins. This was difficult since we didn't know how long the birth mom and Baby were going to be in town and they kept getting shuffled from place to place. And we were simultaneously trying to visit while getting our house ready for a new child. Oh, and I was also still trying to work! I never thought I'd be thankful that I was having such a slow period work-wise, but having sporadic and understanding clients and tonnes of support from my office at this time worked out pretty well. Because truly, it was a bit of a shitshow.

We made ourselves as available as possible for visits. We took birth mom and Baby for lunch, went to parks, toured art galleries, wandered around touristy places, visited with them at the agency, and also in our home. It was suggested by our social worker that we host them for dinner along with my parents. The birth mom had asked to meet them, as they were involved grandparents with my nieces and nephew already and would very much be in baby boy's life.

Now, I try to cook healthy as much as I can. I try to serve meatless dinners once or twice a week, much to my Alberta-born husband's chagrin. This was a bit of a panic though, because the birth mother was vegan. Even my vegetarian meals will sometimes have chicken stock in them, or eggs, a splash of milk, honey etc. So, on top of the general panic and sleeplessly surreal life we were currently living, I was now trying to figure out just HOW vegan she was. If I make my tasty tofu stir fry with rice or quinoa, am I allowed to drizzle my usual bit of honey? Honey comes from bees. Not vegan. Doesn't hurt the bees though, and it's not a living entity itself, so maybe vegan? Her opinion was what mattered. Anyway, she was fine with it, so my non-stop brain calmed down a little and we prepared to host everyone, including Baby, at our home for an evening.

I knew my folks would be amazing, which they were. The food turned out quite well and seemed to go over well (my patient, tofu-hating stepdad even made all of the appropriate yummy noises with a smile on his face). As I hosted, I was thinking how difficult it might be to cook and clean in the future with a baby who doesn't really ever want to be put down, while tripping over the newly acquired baby things that had exploded all over our teeny house. Our life was about to change exponentially. So I was, you know, super calm and collected.

We were also a bit terrified of how things would go when we let our fur-baby Charlie in to meet her potential baby brother.

There was absolutely no need to be nervous! We let her in, and she charged right up to Baby, who was sitting on my lap, sniffed him enthusiastically, and licked his face all over. We all held our breath as Baby took a moment to make a face and look around with a "What the hell was that?!" expression. Then he reached for Charlie's face with his little hands in a moment that felt magical in its ability to completely set us all at ease. Major icebreaker achieved! We all collectively exhaled and had a chuckle. I hadn't realized that my shoulders had been up around my ears until that moment when they deflated back down to a normal position. I wish we had been allowed to take pictures of all of this, but until the twenty-one days were up, no pictures or videos were allowed.

After the dinner and several days spent with the birth mom and Baby, we had a couple of days in which we were allowed to have him dropped off at our house for a few hours so that we could all be alone together. This would help him, and us, to adjust and get used to each other, and help set birth mom at ease that we were capable parents and that he'd be in good hands with us. Fair enough. I am proud to say that we all survived! Despite extreme exhaustion and teething! *self high five

While these visits were monopolizing our days, our evenings were spent working on getting the house ready, working, getting things like groceries, and cramming with baby "how-to" books like our final exam was the next day and we hadn't even cracked the study guide…which was basically true. What do seven- month-olds eat? Should they be napping? How much? How do we begin a routine for someone who's never had one? How do we get him to self-soothe, so that we can put him down once in a while, if he's never had to? When do we introduce certain foods? And on and on and on it went. Then we'd pretend to sleep while our minds went nuts with worry, excitement, list making, and general panic.

We were still unsure what we were supposed to be doing or how we were supposed to be preparing. We had to go and get fingerprinted at the last minute (more ka-ching) because the legislation had changed in the two months since we'd finished our file. Great. We met with our lawyer and gave her the retainer payment (ka-ching). We picked up things from friends that were baby-related. We swapped out furniture for pieces with more storage potential. We Googled. We looked at cribs and car seats, though decided not to buy such things until after the waiting period was over. Best not to spend any more money unless we had to, just in case things fell apart, though things were all going REALLY well and completely on track. In general, we just had to roll with it.

I suck at rolling with it.

The plan changed at least twice a day. It got so that, even though we adore the social workers at the adoption agency, every time they called we would groan because it either meant everything we had planned had been suddenly changed, or more money was needed, or both. That earlier assignation of "DON'T FREAK OUT" to Kyle's phone for the number of the adoption agency continued to be good advice in new and exciting ways. I cancelled meetings and skipped planned gym classes because we couldn't plan farther ahead than a few hours. Our schedule was dictated to us by fitting visits in and jumping through hoops. I supposed I'd have to get used to it though, as parents must roll with it daily...right? Don't answer that. I can't hear you, and you might be talking to yourself in public.

In the midst of all of this, we were obviously becoming more and more attached to Baby, as he was to us. This is the age when attachments are really, really important. We were advised that we should be his caregivers as much as possible during visits, so that he would start to realize that WE were the people who would look after him. We should be the ones to change his diapers, bathe him, feed him, comfort him etc. This should continue after we get him for as long as possible and is called the "cocoon" stage. Even if Grandma comes to visit, we should be the ones to take care of the serious stuff, and we were happy to do it! We finally started to feel like parents. We got to take him to the park and wander around with a stroller, feeling so proud and happy that we were no longer that creepy couple enjoying the park and staring longingly at the beautiful young families that passed us by. We also ran into some friends, who gave me excited, and extremely confused, looks. Awkward! This city is too small sometimes.

In the middle of all of this, I woke up in a cold sweat wondering if I was suddenly, inexplicably pregnant. You hear about couples who can't conceive, then they adopt and BAM!, pregnant. My sense of panic was heightened by the fact that I was late. Like, really late. I was also incredibly stressed, which would explain it, but I had to know. I went to the store and bought what felt like my 412th advance pregnancy test. Not pregnant. Welp! At least now I knew and could move on.

So, the house was ready. We were starting to feel ready and excited. Birth mom was liking us, and Baby was too. I was even able to get him laughing without picking him up! We were in the car: Kyle driving, birth mom in the front passenger seat, and me and Baby in the back. He was exhausted and inconsolable, but I couldn't feed him or hold him since he was in a car seat, so I just made faces and sang to him while keeping my hand on his tummy and stroking his face. He eventually calmed down and was considering sleep. I realize that this was not a prize-winning feat, but I was rather proud of myself! My point is that it was a go. We'd spent ten days with him, and the birth mom was happy with the situation and had even said that we should start calling him by his new name, keeping his birth name as his middle name. Social workers were excited and walked us through the next steps. The next morning our lawyer was going to court to get a judge to grant the waiver, allowing the birth mom to sign the adoption papers and we would have him for our first night and start the twenty-one-day countdown. TOMORROW. Eeeeeeeeee!!!! Parenthood, here we come!!!

Plot Twist

The next morning, I went to the gym for what was theoretically going to be my last class for a while. My close friends at the gym were almost as excited as I was, and it was amazing to have such support. I somehow made it through the class in a daze without hurting myself, and then went to the grocery store downstairs to pick up a few things. Then I got a call.

The judge hadn't granted the waiver.

What?! How? Why?

Apparently, we hadn't tried hard enough to serve the biological father, and should try doing so through Facebook. Facebook? Seriously? WE DIDN'T KNOW WE COULD DO THAT! SO much money and time could have been saved! So much stress could have been avoided!

Anyway, the lawyer and the people at our adoption agency, together with birth mom, made it happen, and he was "served" that day through the marvels of social media messaging. But we weren't going to get our boy that day; the law apparently indicated that Baby couldn't be placed until five business days after the online "serving." One of my best friends found me vibrating/crying/dazedly looking at organic cereals in the supermarket and came running for comfort. Once again, thank God for good friends and family. These new developments were stressful, expensive, and threw off our whole newly planned schedule—I had arranged to be alone with Baby while Kyle would be back in school by the time placement happened. But whatever, still going to be parents! We'd figure it out!

I should say that Kyle and I have this thing where when things don't go as planned, or seem to suck, or the world is seemingly hellbent on kicking us in the teeth, we shout, "PLOT TWIST!" and try to move on. (Yeah, theatre people are weird sometimes. We're cool with it.) So...

PLOT TWIST!!

That night while we were licking our wounds at home and trying to figure out how things were going to look now, how much more money this was going to take etc., we got another call. "DON'T FREAK OUT." Yeah, right. (Our relationships with our phones at this point were tumultuous at best.)

The proverbial shit hit the fan. We were all completely gobsmacked at the way things were unfolding and at the likelihood that we probably weren't going to get to parent this beautiful child after all. Baby's estranged family had intervened. Sometimes the system is…messed up. Maybe unfair is a better term? Sure. Let's go with that. Unfair. What we, birth mom, the lawyers, and the agency had worked for and all believed was best for this child (and birth mom) wasn't what the court heard or granted.

After some more visits, lots of crying, and lots of thinking, birth mom and Baby were going to have to go back home and we'd let all of our lawyers try to figure things out. We were all still on board, birth mom included, so we'd try to navigate the laws and system as best we could. The first court date was still over a month away as in birth mom's rural community they only had court one day per month.

We went to have another visit with birth mom and Baby, knowing that it might well be our last. The drive and walk up to the hotel where they were staying seemed like slow motion. It was like moving through molasses, while also floating and being detached all at once. We walked up to their room door, and when we walked in, Baby turned to us, grinned, and reached out for us. This is something that will be burned into my memory forever, because

1. it was heart-wrenchingly beautiful, and everything that I had ever wanted. And
2. because I knew this could be the last time we would be together like this; our last time to see him. Ever.

We held him and played his favourite "games", twirling him in the air until he cackled with complete glee, and did the "horsey ride" my parents did with me, where you bounce the baby on your knee while singing "this is the way the ladies ride," then you speed up and sing about the gentlemen, then, even faster, "the jockeys." He loved it. We hugged birth mom, and we all tried to keep our brave and optimistic faces on, but the heartbreak in the room was palpable. She was trembling, and I tried to comfort her and tell her it would all be okay when I myself really had no idea if it was true.

Time passed by far too quickly in this brief, potentially final, meeting. We gathered ourselves and had some last words of comfort and encouragement, and then went to leave. We turned and walked out of the room, down the hall, and into the elevator. As soon as the elevator door closed on Kyle and me, we held each other and wept. We were gutted. We had waited and worked all of our lives for this. We were so close to being parents, and had gone through ALL of the things—hoops, various emotional roller coasters, and now THIS was happening?! Unreal. We had grown so attached to him, and he to us, and now he was gone from our lives and we might never see him again. Would we see his grin that went from ear to ear again? Would he reach for us when we walked into the room next time? Would he remember us next time? Would there even *be* a next time? This wee little man had our hearts completely in his grip, and in such a short amount of time!

And just as suddenly, he was gone.

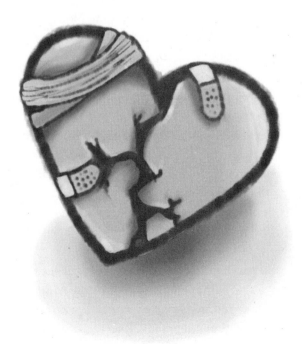

We all had a month to wait, and to think. It felt like a year. Birth mom was doing the best she could, with absolutely no support. We couldn't even provide comfort or much contact, as we didn't want her to feel, or for it to look like, we were trying to influence her or her decisions. After everything that she had gone through, and then waiting even longer and dealing with court proceedings, maybe she would just decide to keep him, and who could possibly blame her? She kept assuring us that she still wanted us to parent this child, and she thought it would work out, but at this point we were tied up in so many knots, and had been on this crazy train of emotion for so long that we were afraid to be too optimistic. We still hoped, but some days more than others. Some days it was almost easier to just believe that it wasn't going to happen and try to suck it up and move on with life. It'd be a hell of a month.

To help distract ourselves (and to heal), we went camping. Every year for our wedding anniversary, Kyle and I take our dog camping for a few days. It's become a lovely tradition that we hope to keep up throughout the years. We had booked our favourite site, right on the water, in a gorgeous campground about three hours away, months in advance. We had cancelled it when we found out that we would be brand-spanking-new parents at that time. Then, when everything hit the fan, we decided to check to see if any sites were still available. As it turned out, that same site was still unbooked! We jumped on it and packed up to get the hell out of our lives for a few days and enjoy some nature-time. This was the BEST decision we could've made. Even though it was only for three days, it was so necessary for helping us to heal, be thankful for the wonderful things that we have in our lives, and gain some perspective. There's nothing quite like sitting around a campfire in the woods, gazing up at the myriad stars above, to make you feel small and like your problems really aren't the end of the world. We swam (well, I swam, and tried to get Charlie the dog to join me), we ate too much, had a few drinks, read our books, and tried to relax and breathe a bit. On the third day we grudgingly packed up and started the drive home, armed with new feelings of rest and hope for whatever future lay ahead.

Five minutes out of the campground, OF COURSE, we got a text from birth mom saying that things were going well with her lawyer. She and Baby were doing fine, and she was still on track to get this kid back into our lives! Cue the resurrection of hope that simultaneously feels great and invigorating, while also terrifying and almost anger-inducing. The roller coaster goes down, aaaaaand the roller coaster goes back up! Food that I ate while camping went down…aaaaaand food that I ate tried to come back up! Hope can be a dangerous thing. It can make you strive for better and do things that you may have thought you couldn't do, and that's wonderful. Hope gives you a reason to get out of bed in the morning and pushes people to do and create incredible things. But it can also be a son-of-a-bitch that sets you up for disappointment. If you never get your hopes up in the first place, then the colossal "thud" of crashing down when things don't work out isn't so brutal.

We had just become comfortable again with the idea that we would be okay without kids. We started to daydream about things we could do, like save up some money and get on a plane somewhere, or maybe just avoid people with children altogether by finding work exchange programs and living life as global explorers. We may have chosen to look forward to these things simply to have SOMETHING to look forward to; a reason to go on. But now we were back to getting excited for a Christmas with a wee boy of our own to introduce to visiting family with their beautiful children. We were back to planning how work schedules would work and how we'd pay off the debilitating debt we were about to significantly increase. We were hopeful and excited once again! It was terrifying.

I found out from some friends who work in "the biz" that apparently this type of eleventh-hour intervention is more common than we had thought, and that, more often than not, the original plan ends up being what happens. We might yet get to parent this child. Birth mom just had a heck of a lot to do in the meantime. This girl, guys. This girl is so strong, and our hearts just went out to her. This young woman is so incredibly brave, and stronger than she will ever know.

Things continued to go up and down in true roller coaster fashion, with hope rising some days, and crashing down the next. We worried, we talked about all of the different possibilities that could happen, and then we sort of became numb. For the most part. We were ready if we got him, but we'd survive if we didn't. If we didn't, we would use whatever credit we had left to take off to somewhere warm over Christmas again, and that would make it easier and give us something to look forward to.

But we couldn't book anything, or plan anything, because we still had no bloody idea what was going to happen.

The numb thing helped a great deal. Things mostly returned to life as we knew it and negative thoughts faded a bit. After all, we told ourselves, it had been only two weeks of our lives that we had known him and had this whirlwind. It all started to feel like some sort of nightmarish dream, except for when reality slapped us awake and reminded us that this was our life, for now anyway. It was like trying to sleep or get anything useful done while ignoring the fact that a super irritating mosquito is just always there, buzzing around your head.

Then a couple of weeks later, I had a bad day.

I got a notification on my phone that morning that I'd forgotten I had programmed. This would've been the twenty-one-day graduation—we would've officially become parents today. My calendar alarm went off with "OFFICIAL PARENTHOOD!" splashed across the screen. Oy. Well THAT was a bit of a gut-punch. I went directly to the gym to blow off some steam, and one of my dearest gym buddies, who knew everything that was happening with us, and had been a HUGE help to us in prepping for this kid, had something that she had to tell me that broke her heart to do so. She was pregnant with their second child.

I burst into tears. I was trying to get the voice to tell her that this was wonderful news, that I was so happy for her! They'd had a loss a few months earlier, and this was truly a blessing for them. What came out were tears and some garbled words that I'm not sure she understood. I'm not sure I understood, either. Sobbing and trying to get my shit together in a public gym washroom before a combat class wasn't something I'd ever done, but hey, new experiences…yay? I don't think I've ever punched and kicked so hard. I almost barfed. I did barf in my mouth a few times, but needed to push through it. I don't know why I'm proud of that, but I am. #gymgoals? Is pushing so hard you puke a gym goal? It can't be a healthy one, but the boost that it gave my mental health was good.

It goes without saying that this was a rough time. Kyle is an amazing partner and always tries to help me look for things to be thankful for. One of the things we focussed on was that the reversal didn't happen AFTER Baby had placement with us. If the judge had granted our waiver, we would've been spending our first night with our son, only to have the RCMP show up and take him away from us without much of an explanation. We would have been celebrating our first night with our kid. This would've added SEVERAL more thousands of dollars to our legal fees, which were already way beyond our reach, or what we'd been told to prepare for. There's no way. It would've finished us financially, and emotionally.

We were also grateful for our friends and family. That night, we had some visitors. One friend stopped by literally just to bring us dinner and a hug because "you're not cooking on a day like today." Amazing. Another couple of friends showed up on my doorstep holding a new bottle of scotch, which they presented to me like a trophy. So on the day we were to get our training wheels on to become parents, we instead got scotch, dinner, and a reminder to count the blessings that we DO have. Consolation prizes aren't the same as winning but truly, my friends and family are the best. I don't have the words to describe how much I love my village of people. Mostly.

The thing is, life doesn't stop just because you want or need it to. People die, relationships break up, hearts are broken, your local grocery store stops carrying your favourite cereal or coffee, and yet you're expected to be cheery and provide good work and comfort to others at all times.

Nobody likes a gloomy Gus, and we felt that everyone expected us to get on with our lives. But we were falling apart inside. And we were broke. Broken AND broke. Great combo. Some people don't let you mourn or be sad. Ever. Others bring you food and scotch (gold stars to those people!). They all have their place, I suppose. It's all support, in one way or another, but sometimes you need to honour your feelings of pain before you can move on. I do think that we should all try to be a little more positive to bring about what we want in life. However, sometimes shit just sucks, and it's hard to move past that if you just ignore it and "keep thinking positive." #Gratitude #Blessed #BlowItOutYourEar

It's important to acknowledge feelings of sadness or pain, just as it's important to focus on the bright side and move forward. We can't have the light without the darkness, people! Negative feelings, especially after a traumatic loss or significant heartbreak, if not acknowledged, can become poisonous. If you don't allow the mourning process of saying to your sadness "I see you. Have a seat, but you can't stay forever," it could impede your actual happiness and forward momentum in future. Listen to Billie Holiday's "Good morning, heartache," or watch *Inside Out*, for example. There's some serious wisdom there.

We really do get how lucky we are in many other ways. We have wonderful friends and family, a loving marriage, the best dog in the world, our health, a roof over our heads, and we live in a free country—among many other blessings. However, right at that moment, we were in pain.

I'm lucky in that my clients and friends usually prefer that I'm a real, live person. I work hard, I'm diligent, and I try to be upbeat and fun to work with and be around, but sometimes I have bad days. You know, like humans do. Truly connecting with people, in my mind, doesn't involve never showing who you really are.

There are places and times of course, but sometimes you just need to vent, amiright? I know people who vent all of the time, especially on social media, and no one tells them to suck it up; but it seems that the second I post anything displaying anything but humour or happiness, I get slammed with comments to the contrary. Okay. Fair enough. I have learned that Facebookland is a place where you only post your best moments, goofy comic shares, or semi-sarcastic things that have a funny spin on them. Or terrifying articles about politics or the environment. Or videos about cats, for some reason. Or puppies. Cats and puppies are allowed.

I had learned this lesson and had been trying to keep my chin up for months. I even had people coming up to me to tell me how much they loved my posts, and how funny I was.

It's great that everyone is finding happy moments in their lives to find their #blessed #gratitude living, but sometimes we're just not okay and I think it's alright, nay, important, to reach out in those times. Sometimes faking it for the social media highlight reel is just exhausting and we don't wanna. Or doing the whole "How's it goin'?" "Good, you?" Canadian greeting. I mean, if I am in the middle of a super shite day, regurgitating the "Good, you?" seems so fake. But responding with "Horrible! But I digress. This was just a greeting, so...good, you?" would probably be met with some raised eyebrows at the very least. Also, everyone's fighting their own battles, and hearing about your crappy day may not be the best thing for that person who was just trying to say hello.

So, fair enough. Time and place. I'm not saying that we should be Eeyore all of the time, but bottling it all up and constantly pretending everything is okay can't be good for us either.

Here's an example: One Sunday morning, Kyle and I were trying to sleep in. We had earned it. It'd been one hell of a couple of months and we thought we were entitled to some rest and healing. We had been up late the night before, having a bonfire, chatting, and generally feeling happy again for what felt like the first time in ages. At 6 a.m. we were awakened by the most INCREDIBLY LOUD squirrels you've ever heard, having some sort of Jerry Springer-type argument directly outside our window. I can't even explain how freakishly loud it was, folks. I got up, made coffee, and made some sort of goofy comment about it on my Facebook feed while I had my breakfast. I even used the squirrel language from *The Emperor's New Groove*, thinking I was putting an adorable spin on a slightly cranky post.

It wasn't long before I got a private message from an acquaintance.

> 6:00am. So you got to sleep in then?
> Oh, right,
> You don't have kids yet.
> Enjoy!

I think that she was genuinely trying to be funny and of course meant no harm. We as humans can say some really stupid things to each other, and the number of appalling things that have been said to me and to just about every person I know going through this struggle is staggering. This kind of thing can sour a whole day or week. This also happened fairly soon after our adoption reversal, and our wounds were still fresh. She couldn't have known that, but that's the thing—you often *never* know what someone else is going through, so you've really got to consult your brain before making a joke sometimes. I should say "we" because I'm sure I've been guilty of this as well. I respect wanting to connect and thinking you're funny, but this is the type of crushing comment that can cut deep. If someone has wrestled with the choice and decided (or the universe decided for them) that having a family is not for them, then being constantly reminded of it is heartbreaking and incredibly insensitive. Being tired is not an "us versus them" thing, reserved only for parents.

Infertility is all kinds of debilitating and adoption is a brutal process that left us feeling completely scraped raw, without any guarantees or end in sight. I still cried every single month when I discovered that I was, yet again, not pregnant. I still cringed every time I seemed to be surrounded by glowing pregnant ladies at the coffee shop, gym, grocery store, park. I still comforted friends who needed to terminate pregnancies that they just couldn't bring themselves to carry, and I was glad to be there for them, but that didn't make it any easier.

So, why the disconnect? Why do people get so uncomfortable with other people's rough times? Does it remind us of our own problems? Or maybe it makes us feel better about our lives, but then bad about ourselves for feeling better about our lives at someone else's expense? Cuz schadenfreude? Maybe we all really want to "fix it," but when faced with a situation we can't fix, we just get super uncomfortable. Sometimes all we need is a "Wow, that sucks." Just be in the moment with us and remind us that we're loved and not alone. Then we can move on!

One particular day recently, I wasn't okay. I couldn't find the energy to pretend to be okay, and I needed to reach out for some support. I also didn't want to be super overshare-y about it, and I knew it wasn't forever; I just wanted comfort. So I made a post on Facebook that simply said: "Bad day. Send GIFs." I KNEW my community of people would provide, and they did not disappoint. I haven't even seen some of these people in over ten years, but they still posted goofy things to make me smile. A lot of them. It was glorious. Because I used to work in theatre and the arts, I know some fabulously creative and funny people. Some of the things they came up with were absolutely off the wall, and I got messages from other people telling me how awesome my friends are. DAMN STRAIGHT! Some people were also having rough days, and the huge thread of ridiculousness made them feel better just to have it come across their feed. It was the gift that kept on giving! Did this fix my problems? Of course not. But these people took time to make me giggle and to remind me that

1. there's a whole world out there bigger than my bad day, and
2. I am so lucky to have them in my life.

Part
3

Fearing Hope

About a year later, I started falling into a trap that Kyle and I swore we would never fall into again: I felt hopeful. Hope can be a wonderful thing that makes us strive for better and look forward, but can also lead to huge, crashy, let-downs. We'd found it much safer and happier to just enjoy life as it is, count our blessings, and we became accustomed to the idea that we wouldn't have children. We were still on the adoption list, and we still "tried" each month, but we just found it safer to assume that nothing would happen. Unless it did. In which case, YAY! But it wouldn't. And that's okay. Unless it did…

We still had fun! It's not like we lived mopey lives that would put Squidward to shame. For heaven's sake, I walked my dog in an inflatable T-Rex costume! It's just with regards to all things baby that we erred on the side of caution.

But then I had new reason to wonder if we might manage to knock me up after all. I had a few friends who'd gone to an amazing endocrinologist for help with depression, insomnia, hair loss, and in some cases, infertility. Because the human body is a finely tuned machine and if one system isn't running smoothly, it can mess up the whole works.

I got a referral to see this unicorn endocrinologist and eagerly awaited my life-changing appointment. She was two hours late, so I was dehydrated and full-on Joe-Pesci-Hangry when I finally got in, but then she spent over an hour with me and was SO COMPLETELY WORTH THE WAIT. Within two minutes of meeting me she told me I have really big, bright eyes…but it didn't feel like a compliment. She said it wasn't, and it's abnormal and a sign of some sort of deficiency. She also said I was puffy and had dry skin. So we were off to a nice start.

She was incredibly intense. She basically opened up a firehose of information onto me and I did my best to pay attention and follow along without getting overwhelmed. I may have failed somewhat...but I nodded a lot!

Before I even went to see her, I was sent a stack of forms to fill out with in-depth family histories of illnesses, and a requisition to get eight vials of blood taken and tested for all sorts of things. At our meeting, she pulled out the pages and pages of my results, as well as blood tests dating back ten years. As it turns out, I have hypothyroidism, and am severely deficient in Vitamin D, B12, and iron (despite doing my best to take vitamins and eat well etc.). I'm also prone to hormone imbalance—gee, go figure. Another thing she mentioned is that in North America the standards for these tests are extremely outdated, so I was remaining unnoticed/undiagnosed because my levels were squeaking by under the standards for healthy levels in Canada and the US. She looked me square in the face and said, "If you lived in Paris, this would've been caught years ago." She also said that (among the laundry list of other symptoms of hypothyroidism that I have) this is ABSOLUTELY why I haven't gotten pregnant, and that we'd fix that and I'd "be pregnant by Christmas." I…wait…WHAT?!

She then asked me how old I was (thirty-five) and legit blurted out "OH MY GOD, YOU ARE THE PERFECT AGE TO GET PREGNANT!"

Then my head exploded. I tried to remain composed while tears rolled down my face because all I've ever heard is how old I'm getting, and how my window is closing etc.

I left on a cloud and promptly called my closest friends and my mom to blubber about all of this. I also went to get my prescriptions so that I could start taking them immediately.

The difference was staggering.

Truly, I didn't realize that I felt crappy until I felt freaking FANTASTIC! I felt more awake and alert. Like, I've always kinda had a shite memory, but I sort of assumed that that was just normal for a busy adult—too many pages open on the toolbar that is my brain. Once my meds kicked in though, it's like I didn't realize that I'd been living in a perpetual fog for years and years. It was so much easier to stay upbeat and positive. My hair loss, depression, weight issues, insomnia, shoulder and hip issues and even my infertility seem to now have an explanation that didn't involve masking symptoms. I'm just deficient in a bunch of vitamins and hypothyroid. Even my gym classes are easier! EU-FREAKING-REKA!

I discovered that thyroid issues, autoimmune disorders, and in some cases, sensitivities to certain foods for certain people can have a HUGE impact on fertility. I was mentioning this to some family members, and they chimed in to reveal the fact that, apparently, autoimmune issues are common on my dad's side of the family, and thyroid issues are common on my mom's side. WOT?! I had no idea. Thirty-five years with these people…I feel like a moron.

Anyway! This was exciting to me. At the very least I'd discover more about myself, and how to treat my body right. Maybe my own bouts of insomnia and former battles with depression would finally be explained! Maybe I'd be told that I'm actually allergic to gluten, lactose (and all things that taste good) like half of my family. Don't worry, folks: in preparation for this possibility, I'd been dutifully stuffing my face with ALL of the baked goods like it was my last chance to do so. (I'm a do-er, ya know!)

I tried hard not to let myself get too excited, but maybe, just maybe, my infertility would finally be explained, and a potential to "fix it" would show itself. I knew it was a long shot, but it was our last (biological) shot, in our minds. Other than IVF, we'd tried everything. I did rigorous acupuncture for months and months, I took so many special Chinese herbs and SUPER GROSS teas I was afraid to yawn for fear that I'd lose some of them like an overflowing pot. I tried the ridiculous post-coital yoga positions to increase my chances. I tried listening to everyone's advice to "just relax." We went on vacations, had spa days, took up meditation again (which is amazing anyway, whether or not you're trying to conceive), took fertility-inducing yoga classes. But other than some interesting experiences, pulled muscles, footprints on the bedroom walls, and well-used travel points and credit cards, all of this did nothing for us in the way of baby-making.

So, despite the fact that we knew that we'd be fine if we never had children and were moving forward with plans assuming that we wouldn't, I couldn't help but feel hope rising up in me again. I loved it and hated it all at once. I'd catch myself imagining having a test come back positive for once, or baby showers, or first words, first steps. Even just having the time to prepare instead of living in limbo and waiting for a phone call that could change our lives in twenty-four hours was appealing.

But what if it was nothing? What if it turned out to be another dead end? Maybe I was just not meant to conceive, and that was okay too. It had to be. I'd cry, then I'd move on and be happy in other aspects of life.
But still. What if…?

Relapse

For the first time in a year, we had hope that we might get to be parents, and the old-fashioned way to boot! I learned so much from this doctor about myself that my head was still spinning. I was feeling good, we felt happy, and we were hopeful again.

There's that bloody word again. Hope.

Dr. Amazing's confidence and excitement was contagious. Anyone who meets with her and experiences her passion and explanations of why bodies do (or don't do) the things that they do can't help but get swept up in it. Add to that the fact that I felt such a palpable difference since meeting with her and you've got one hopeful Wenna! This is what I tried to explain to Kyle when he urged me not to get too excited or hopeful again. I spent years getting my hopes up every single month only to be crushed.

For the most part we had gotten pretty good at not caring or being quite as broken each month when Herman brought the "red tide" as Kyle called it. Kyle also came up with Herman, the angry dwarf who lives trapped in a jar inside of my uterus who, once a month, breaks free and wreaks havoc with his battle-axe. This is Kyle's inventive explanation for my cramps and other symptoms and is completely irrelevant to the story except for the fact that I find it hilarious, and it's much more fun to get mad at Herman once a month instead of our own perceived failings at conceiving.

For years, whenever our hearts hurt from Herman destroying our hopes and dreams with his axe, Kyle would take me for sushi. (Sushi is a no-no when you're pregnant, so it's a nice consolation prize). We used to go to the same place and order a party platter for two-three people, which Kyle nicknamed "The Period Platter." Once, a friend was

mentioning that restaurant to me as a great place she had gone recently. Before thinking, I blurted "Oh yeah! We love that place! We go there for the Period Platter." The horrified look on her face was FANTASTIC, and I had to quickly explain that no, it is not an actual menu item (ew, can you imagine? No wait, don't.) and just something that we say when we go for sushi as a consolation prize for not being pregnant yet again.

We went back to "actively trying," as opposed to just living our lives and hoping for the best, but being okay if things didn't happen. So we tried. Again. A lot. (Heheheheh. *Winks and high-fives Kyle*). The first month's visit from Herman was disappointing, but we thought "Okay! That's fair, it can take more than a few weeks for my body to adjust to the new drugs, hormones, and vitamins." The second month I wasn't so level-headed. In fact, truth be told, I was completely heartbroken.

This time, about two weeks before my period was due, my breasts started to hurt. Like, A LOT. Sometimes that happens, but not two weeks early like this, and not this bad! Don't touch them. Don't breathe on them. Don't even look at them or think of them. On top of that, I was nauseous for over a week and felt beyond exhausted. I was so tired that at three separate times during a twenty-minute walk with my dog, I felt like I needed to stop to rest or maybe take a nap in a snowbank. How could I NOT get my hopes up?!

So, after days of agonizing and wondering and hoping and then chastising myself for said hope, I took an early-detect pregnancy test. NOT PREGNANT. Again. Ever. FFS.

By now, I'd taken so many pregnancy tests that this shouldn't faze me. This time, however, I was a DISASTER. I don't know if it was the renewed hope, the sure belief that this time would be different, or the new hormone levels having party time in my body. Maybe I was fighting a flu. Maybe it was all of the above. At any rate, I was a wet mess.

I walked the dog, fighting tears all the way. I got home to grab my gym bag and headed out to a class and foolishly ran to pull the test out of the garbage just in case it had needed a little more time to change its mind. #dumbass I'm an idiot. I knew better than this, but six of my friends were pregnant, and several others had just had beautiful babies. I had been allowing myself to dream again of future Christmases with an excited little one, birthdays, coming home from a long day and having someone's face light up and squee "Mommy!" before reaching for me.

I then drove to the gym, crying all the way. To be fair, having the *Dear Evan Hansen* soundtrack on in my car MAY have been a bad contribution to this little soap opera. #allthefeels So, after providing entertainment at stoplights while sob-singing to "You Will Be Found," I got to the gym locker room just in time to hear some ladies I knew talking about being moms and how some ladies they knew had trouble getting pregnant. I fell apart. Again. Cuz, apparently, that's what was going to happen that day. It was like a relapse back to where I was two or three years before.

I got my shit together to take a class, went home, worked from home via phone and email for the day while repeatedly bursting into tears while inwardly laughing at how ridiculous I was being at the same time.

That evening I got comfort from Kyle, and a reminder that we'd be okay if we never had kids, that I was enough for him. Herman had also arrived, and with that, my emotions returned to normal. We found ourselves a little ticked at Dr. Amazing for getting our hopes up again and for making promises. No doctor should make promises. Just in general. I still loved her for her knowledge and unwavering desire to help people. I just had to choose not to believe her hype for now, for self-preservation. Maybe we'd get a lovely surprise and prove her right, but for now we'd just have to wait and see what happened.

Weaponized Sperm

We have a lovely friend who is a doctor. He lives far away, and we rarely get to see him, but he still tries to be helpful, as good friends do. While both Kyle and I had been repeatedly checked out over about four years to see why we couldn't conceive, we wanted to just check Kyle's…er…swimmers out one more time. The lab and doctor said we'd get the results in three days, but it took over a month for Kyle to hunt down his results and find that he has a low sperm count. Coupled with my hypothyroidism that makes us just the perfect storm for infertility. #overachievers Our lovely doctor friend said that we should still keep trying, and suggested a regimen of vitamins for Kyle to try that would "weaponize his sperm."

THE SPERMINATOR

After I finished laughing, we set about ordering them to give this a try.

The truth is that this doctor had actually gently recommended this list of supplements over a year before, but Kyle being the dude that he is, never really committed to taking them. After seeing our friend at Christmas and having him use the term "weaponized sperm" and being reminded just how much shit *I've* been through, he decided that it was worth a shot. This is not to disparage my incredible husband; life is busy, and the adoption and infertility journey is exhausting and all-consuming, and sometimes it's hard to be motivated to get back on the crazy train after four years of let-downs. Personally, I think that it was the language used that did it. *Weaponized sperm* does seem pretty badass, no?

Now that both of us had a better idea of how our bodies did and didn't work, we figured we'd give "trying" to get pregnant one last try. If that didn't work out, then we'd return to our earlier decision to not have kids and *need* to be okay with it. In the meantime, we'd stay on the adoption list as well. If we ended up getting a nice surprise, great, but trying and getting our hopes up each month like we had been for *years* was exhausting and emotionally excruciating. After four years of this shit and nine more friends currently pregnant—we needed to be done. We needed to heal and let it go instead of holding onto something that was only causing pain and extra stress. I needed to be able to be around my friends and their bellies and their kids without dying inside. I wanted to be a part of their lives without making excuses for being absent or plastering a smile on my face and faking my way through a visit.

One of the ways that we coped was by LIVING OUR LIFE. We moved to a larger home closer to Kyle's work. We had date nights. We sometimes went to movies and out to dinner on short notice. We traveled. We blew money on things like T-Rex suits and games. We did the things that wouldn't be so easy with a baby or kids in our lives. We're only on this earth for so long, so should we be wasting our time here sitting home and feeling sorry for ourselves, or should we try to go out in search of a giggle when our hearts hurt.

Kyle

As Morwenna and I explore a few new avenues to possibly become parents, there are some areas that Morwenna can't really write about because they focus on the male experiences in the process. For example, providing a semen sample.

There were two ways presented to me to drop off a sample for my doctor to analyze: the first, create my sample at home and then drop it off within thirty minutes; the second, go to their clinic and create the sample there and then leave. The first time I went through the process, right at the beginning of our fertility journey, I opted to create my sample at home and then drop it off at the clinic. So, in the comfort of my own home, I played scientist and then dropped off the sample.

I have had a history of seeing a few of what I shall refer to as "educational videos" that are available on the internet, but I understood that these might have left me with an incredibly incorrect and skewed understanding of what a normal volume of semen looks like from an ejaculation. So, when comparing these educational videos to my own sample creations, I was concerned. I had this little cup to "fill," and I didn't even cover the bottom. I dropped off my sample at the lab, concerned that the news that would come back would be bad news. However, I never heard from my doctor to discuss what the results were, and I have always been told that when it comes to doctors, no news is good news. So I continued in my day-to-day life.

After a couple years, the creation of a new sample for analyses was requested, just for comparison. This time, I opted to go into the clinic and take an afternoon off from work. Call me crazy, but heading to school after creating a sample felt a bit weird, and I did not want to do that. I headed down to the clinic for some alone time.

Now this, this was an interesting day. I don't care who you are, walking into a building, approaching the receptionist, and basically saying, "Hi, I'm here to masturbate" is not a cool experience. Sure, these people deal with this hundreds of times a month, but I still see it in their eyes: that whole "I know what you're going to do in that room, you naughty, naughty man."

The clerk took my papers, gave me my love-cup, and took me to a room. Let me set this up right away: whoever designed this particular room has NEVER "provided a sample" before. The room was off the main (very busy) hallway, did NOT have a lock on it, and had (basically) a dentist chair in it for sitting. Also, there was no "research material" provided. So I closed the door and awkwardly sat down. As I tried to focus on the task at hand (pun intended), I couldn't help but hear the people who worked in the building walking and talking right outside my UNLOCKED door. Somehow, I was able to get things done and create a sample. At this point, silly thoughts began to enter my mind. Do I thank them for letting me stay in their room? Do I have to talk to anyone when I leave? Did I take an appropriate amount of time? Suddenly, I was super concerned about the amount of time I should spend in this room. I didn't want to be too quick (because reasons) or look like I was taking too long. I didn't want them to think I was lighting candles and setting the mood, and the last thing I wanted was someone knocking on the door to see if everything was alright. I lingered for what felt like a reasonable amount of time, and then I realized I was being an idiot, and I just left because, surprisingly, I am an adult (by law).

As I was dropping off the sample, I took a look at it and again was a little disappointed with the less-than-a-side-of-ketchup-at-McDonalds amount that was in there. But I'm not a (legal) doctor, so what do I know? The results came back a week or so later, and I phoned my doctor's office for the results.

At no point did my doctor speak to me about these results. The receptionist read the numbers, and I asked what they meant, but she didn't have full understanding. Fair enough. I jotted down the numbers she said and did some Googling.

The Google results were not uplifting. A normal sample can range anywhere between 8–24 million swimmers. Anything below eight is considered low. I came in (hehe) at around four hundred thousand. This was super low and is likely the reason we have not been getting pregnant. I spoke to a friend of mine who is a doctor to discuss the results since my actual doctor didn't seem to have the time. Upon his recommendations, I made some lifestyle changes and began a vitamin regimen that would increase count, motility, and overall libido. I followed this plan for about five months. When asked, my friend did say that with my count where it was, it was unlikely that I would see any significant increase, but every little bit helps. Basically, these vitamins were meant to "weaponize" (doctor's words) my sperm. It's like I have one Commando with all the tactical gear needed to take down a small village. He is: the Sperminator. However, even with the best Commando available, the village is likely to withstand the assault.

So there it is: the uncovered reason why we haven't been getting pregnant. For years, Morwenna has been bullying herself because she believed there was something wrong with her—that she was at fault, somehow, for our struggles. I would always try my best to lift her up and tell her that I married her, not her womb. We would be fine as DINKS (Dual Income No Kids) and have great adventures together. Still, every month when the Red Tide would rise, Morwenna would slip into a sneaky hate spiral. I hate seeing her sad, so I try to honour her feelings and help her through this quagmire of crap life was throwing at us. In the back of my mind, I had this lingering nugget that this was in fact all on me. Now, we know it is.

With this newfound knowledge, I have been guilt-ridden and fighting the ridiculous voice inside my head that is telling me that I am not "a man." Admitting weakness of any kind is tough. Why? I don't know, actually. Maybe it's because I grew up in a time where I was bombarded from the media with the idea that a man is supposed to be strong. That a man is tough. That a man doesn't cry. That a man has a 40 million sperm count, and each sperm swims like Michael Phelps. And if a man is struggling, a man holds it inside.

What garbage.

The rational part of my brain recognizes that all of these ideas are not only foolish, but are truly harmful, to the individual and to our society. But since I was eighteen, I have wanted to be a father. Now Wenna and I are in our last-ditch efforts to try and have children, and we are facing the very real possibility that we might not have kids. And that sucks. It sucks a lot. And, even though I know it's silly, even though I know it has nothing to do with anything I have done or who I am, I can't help but feel responsible for this—that it's somehow my fault.

Morwenna has been outstanding and has been very supportive, telling me all the things that I told her when she was feeling crummy over the last few years: that I am enough for her, that she married me and not my sperm count, and that our lives will be full of laughter and joy, with or without kids. And she's absolutely right. I have to continue to fight this mentality of shame and focus on the positive things in life. I cannot build my entire mental state on my sperm count. I know that whether or not we have kids, Morwenna and I will have a beautiful life together. And although we are facing struggles and problems right now, we will move forward with open minds and open hearts. After all, it is not our problems that define who we are; rather, it's how we face them that matters.

Part

4

Adjusting

We had made the agonizing decision not to continue with the reversed adoption, or rather, not to continue to wait for another couple of years to find out if we'd get the (extremely unlikely) chance to parent that beautiful little boy. We waited another couple of months, with occasional updates of the "well, the first and second court dates didn't go so well," type. We spoke with our lawyer, friends who are lawyers, and other folks with experience in this type of thing, and the general consensus was that this could take years to resolve, and that the likelihood of him being placed with us, after so long apart, was basically nonexistent.

Meanwhile, Baby was healthy. He was growing and forming attachments, and we were missing it all. When we had him, he was about to start crawling at any minute, and was in FULL babble-mode. He wasn't quite saying actual words yet, but it would've been soon. We'd had many conversations—they just weren't in English. Now he was probably talking and walking, and picturing it put a lump in my throat. Though we were still feeling raw with grief, we knew that his birth mother loved him and that ultimately he'd be safe and happy with her. We hoped that her own battles with her parents would be over quickly, and that she and Baby would have a good life.

When we spoke with our social workers to tell them our decision, they completely supported us. This helped immensely. We felt like the worst human beings in the world for walking away, but continuing to live with this agony and uncertainty for another year or two, with an incredibly slim chance of ever getting to adopt this little boy, was just too much for us. The friends and family around us, and the folks at the adoption agency, helped us to feel that we were doing what was right for us, and not to feel guilty. We wrote a letter to Birth Mom explaining our decision, and that it IN NO WAY had anything to do with her or with her perfect son. We thanked her for choosing us, and for the chance we had to get to know them both. We told her how much we admire her and how strong she is, and to never let anyone tell her that she wasn't, and that we wished for nothing but the best for them.

We also temporarily took our file out of "the box" to be considered for adoptions. We needed to let the scab have a chance to really heal. We needed quiet. We needed to figure out what life was again, and we also needed to pay off the financial damages and try to save up again. Even if we had been okay emotionally with being chosen again, and we *were* chosen again, we had nothing left. Well, less than nothing, really. No bank account with the cash needed to pay for this whole process to begin again, and a line of credit that was getting uncomfortably high.

The staff and social workers at the adoption agency were AMAZEBALLS. They were kind, attentive, knowledgeable, and sensitive to what we were feeling, all while remaining professional and appropriately objective. Adoption is incredible, much needed and rewarding. But after feeling like we'd been tossed down a mountain, climbed and clawed our way back up, only to get tossed back down again, we were starting to think it might not be the path for us.

We hid all things baby. We put away the play area we'd built in the living room. We got rid of the stroller by the front door, and the toys, diapers, clothes, baby dishes and baby food from the rest of the main floor. We stashed things in the basement or up in my former office that had since become a nursery. Neither of us entered that room for months. MONTHS. It was just too painful.

The next while was pretty rough. We waffled back and forth between being "Fine. It's fine. Such is life" and "This is Bullshit." We realized that we needed to FEEL this in order to move past it.

In October we stopped trying to deny that we were hurting, which was an interesting experiment. I went camping for a weekend with a volunteer crew I work on for the Winnipeg Folk Festival. I only took a few drinks' worth of alcohol with me and was rather proud of this decision! #adulting

Some friends came out to join us around the fire for a few hours, which was lovely. What was less than lovely (for me) was the fact that the conversation around the fire for well over an hour was all about pregnancy, babies, fertility, and parenting. I swear I didn't bring it up! What I did do was sit quietly while people talked, and a beautiful friend who was aware of my recent situations frantically kept trying to change the subject, to no avail. Kyle texted me to see how things were going, and I mentioned the current fun times I was having. Something really important about this partner of mine is that, despite thinking I'd be a good mother, and that being a factor in his choosing to marry me, he has never made me feel like "less than" if we never end up having kids. I try to do the same for him, but he has a knack for making super grand and moving statements. In this case he just texted (in that handwritten app thingie) "You're Enough." I'm enough for him, just as I am. We are enough together, and we'll have a great life even without children. This prompted some tears, and another lovely friend decided to help me drown my sorrows by continually filling my cup and handing me more booze. SUPER sweet intentions. Not such sweet consequences.

I have never been so inebriated, and I hope never to be so again. I drank my feelings…and I may or may not have gotten feelings all over the place later on. I guess I wasn't as "fine" as I thought I was and numbing things with alcohol seemed like a good idea at the time. BOY WAS THAT WRONG! The next day was brutal. Ten hours of labour outdoors in the rain while more hungover than I had ever been in my life was … less than fun. And embarrassing. I've never been "that girl." What it DID do is act as some sort of catharsis for me, which made me think that perhaps trying to listen to people who basically told me to walk it off, look forward, and be happy might not be the best plan at that moment. Sometimes depression is a filthy liar and has to be ignored lest it get under your skin and destroy you; and sometimes it needs to be embraced in order to move on. Grief is a thing. I needed to honour my feelings and just be in it for a bit in order to get through it.

For Halloween that year we thought it would be funny to represent our view of 2016—as "Sadness" and "Anger" from the movie *Inside Out*. We thought it was funny. Those friends who understood the reference thought it was funny. Others not so much. Some folks told us we should be moving on, not wallowing. This is HOW we were moving on, people! When we start joking around again, you can trust that we're on the right path. We weren't walking around like Eeyore, saying "ERMAHGERD, life sucks so bad." We were just enjoying a private joke while getting compliments on our ridiculous costumes. We were acknowledging things and moving on in our own way. We had an awesome time and had some laughs. Laughter really is a pretty great medicine.

Then in December we decided to do something we like to call "Crispy Christmas." We planned to blow off Christmas entirely and booked a week at a Cuban resort with some friends from Yellowknife to spend a week on the beach. Far away from snow, family (despite much love for family), and friends, with their adorable pregnant bellies, babies, and toddlers running around having the times of their lives—this was heaven and JUST what the doctor ordered.

Then my brother, his wife, and my niece and nephew decided to come in from Alberta and visit for Christmas, which never happens. My mom was ecstatic. She was less thrilled when we announced that we weren't planning to be there. In fact, less thrilled doesn't even scratch the surface. Kyle's folks also weren't happy with the fact that we wouldn't be going to visit them for Christmas for the second year in a row. So, after much facting, figuring, credit card-destroying, and negotiation, we decided to spend Christmas with the family, (Kyle's folks even came HERE for a few days!) and take off first thing on the 27th. "Crispy Christmas" became "Auld Lang Crispy." This was going to be it. This was going to be the break that we needed, the attitude adjustment that would put us back into hopeful and joyous mindsets for the beginning of 2017.

Or not.

Well, let's just say that 2016 went out in the same manner as it had behaved all year. Our friends from Yellowknife got completely dicked around by Air Canada, and lost two days of their vacation, so there was that. Our resort SUCKED! Truly. Extremely rude and unhelpful staff, our room was equipped with brutal beds, a balcony railing that was rotted and falling out of the wall, so unsafe to lean on. We also had mould on our ceiling, our lampshades and furniture seemed to have survived a fire. We had sharp, rusty patches on our bathtub, missing tiles, broken furniture, and the loudest hallway ever.

Some of the dancing was cool, though, the booze flowed freely, the coffee bar was THE BEST THING EVER, and the beaches were absolutely beautiful. So who cares! Eventually our friends arrived, and we settled in to squeeze every drop of fun out of this trip if it killed us.

Then, right on cue, Kyle got what was most likely E. coli. Which makes sense as we saw some super sketchy food-handling going on, and literal flocks of birds hanging out on the buffets. On them. Like, directly on the food. What's funny, but not really, is I had mostly veggies, salads, and lots of chicken and seafood, while Kyle stuck to potatoes, bread, pasta, and beef to AVOID GETTING SICK.

My poor guy had the most horrid four days stuck in our gross room, while urging me to try to enjoy the trip and get our money's worth on behalf of both of us. His stomach was so distended that he looked about seven months pregnant. He blew through all of the Imodium and Pepto we had brought and couldn't seem to find help in our resort medical centre.

He gave himself a pep talk into the mirror on New Year's Eve. Stared himself down seriously and said "Kyle. You can do this. Don't poop for one hour. Have a nice dinner with your wife and friends, kiss her, and come back to bed. This will not beat you." It worked. He came out, plastered a smile on his face, picked at his dinner, watched some of the "show" (such as it was), kissed me Happy New Year, and went back to bed. He fought bravely. On the morning of New Year's Day, he woke up feeling much better and was able to have an actual meal and leave the resort. So 2016 sucked right up until the last possible second, but 2017 literally had a whole different feeling! Bring on some better times!

We had a few more less-than-awesome experiences on our trip, but what I can say is that it fixed "us." We were back in sync with each other and looking forward with a new hope for the first time in ages. It felt like a massive weight was lifting off of our chests. We were still hurt, and terrified that we would suffer an adoption reversal again, but we decided to get back on the crazy train. We called the adoption agency in January to ask them to reopen our file for prospective birth mothers to choose from.

Looking Forward

We had been through fire and come out on the other side. Good for us. Now, we were back on the adoption "list" and trying to figure out just how this was going to work with the mountain of debt still weighing on our minds (and credit) and my work situation was still less than stellar. We had no idea where the money would come from, but we decided that we couldn't give up. To make things easier, I moved brokerages for work to one that has a different fee structure.

Our financial situation slowly got much better, which took a huge load off. Hope is great, but if general life costs are out of reach, then financing your aspirations and dreams is something that seems about as likely as going from beer-league hockey to the pros in your forties? (I'm sorry, Kyle, it's just not going to happen). We weren't rolling in it by any means, but back on navigable footing, which just made everything seem brighter.

Whenever prospective parents go through a reversal and wish to go back in "the box" for adoption, they have to go in and meet with their social worker again to check in and talk about how things are going, and how they feel going forward.

Makes total sense.

I did not want to do it.

The reason I didn't want to do it was that I was still so full of anger, pain, and resentment that I was afraid it would come across during the interview. I didn't think that I would *really* be judged for my feelings, but I didn't think it would look terribly good if I were spitting venom and tears while simultaneously asking to be handed another baby. We decided that Kyle should do the majority of the talking and I would sit quietly and nod.

Which, of course, didn't happen at all.

We went in for our meeting, and it was fine. Actually, it was better than fine, and I'm so glad we went. After months of feeling shitty and being told by many loving friends and family members to "just let it go" and "move on" we were starting to feel silly for still being so upset, wondering if we were just being melodramatic and should just get over ourselves already. Our social worker was so sympathetic and reassured us that what we had been through was, in fact, HUGE, and not something that can easily be brushed off.

This is the stuff that destroys marriages. So the fact that the worst we ever got was out of sync and on each other's nerves spoke well of our relationship, and we felt rather proud of ourselves. Hearing that what we had been feeling was completely normal, having it be acknowledged, and also hearing that our social workers and our lawyer all still talked about this case as being one of the worst they had ever seen, made me feel oddly better. I think that was something that I needed in order to truly move forward with hope (and crippling fear, but…you know… potayto, potahto).

Things were looking up, which wasn't to say that I was suddenly all sunshine and happiness. Some days I was fine, even happy, confident that even if I didn't ever have kids, I'd have a great life: we'd be that cool couple that travels and stays up late and goofs off with our friends' kids. Then I'd go for a stroll to a local bakery and see all of the lovely pregnant ladies out for a walk, or the young moms out with their babies, enjoying the sunshine and fresh air, and I'd have to run to my car so I didn't burst into tears in line for a single muffin. It's a roller coaster.

One thing we had been doing for self-preservation was avoiding the nursery upstairs altogether. I went up there to make the bed for my in-laws when they came for Christmas, but other than that we generally avoided that room. But then that friend of mine who'd told me that she was pregnant with her second child was approaching her due date, so she'd be needing her loaned clothing and baby items back. It was time to re-enter the "forbidden lands." *Cue dramatic theme music*

I had put all of our wonderful donations and gifts all together, so one shelf was full of onesies, one had pants, one had sweaters etc. Luckily, this friend had labelled all of her stuff, so all I had to do was search through

it all. Fun times. It only took me about four tissues and one rather strong old fashioned to do it. Nowhere near the entire box of tissues and bottle of bourbon I had expected. #growth #kidding #wellkindakidding

Honestly though, I had been dreading that day, and while it wasn't a day at the spa, it wasn't as bad as I thought it would be. Good indicator that my heart was healing. #babysteps #toosoon? #probablytoosoonforababystepsjoke

I was ready to take our baby journey on a new path.

A Completely Different Life 2001–2002

He made me sleep on the floor, which was filthy. Under a table. A mouse ran by once.

I suppose he never "made" me do anything. I am my own woman, though at the time I was only nineteen. He was ten years my senior and had seemed so amazing in the beginning.

There was an alarm bell that was pretty much always going off in the back of my mind for that year, but sometimes it really was logical to just let him win and stay over, knowing that I couldn't sleep in the bed. His knee hurt, you see. Having me in the bed made it worse. It also made it harder for him to sneak out of bed and into my purse to swipe my bank card to rob me blind, but it makes no matter now.

I was working multiple jobs while also attending university. I needed my sleep, and I would get more sleep on a dingy floor in a rooming house than I would if I went home. If I went home, he would call, every hour on the hour, to make sure I was home and not out with someone else. Like I would ever! If I unplugged my phone he would come over and wake the whole house. Using my family against me was one of his best tools.

I was embarrassed, terrified, hurt, and believed that I deserved no better than this. Much later, I learned how abusers work: isolating their victims from friends and family to make them easier to manipulate, convincing them that they are lucky to have this relationship, this person who cares so much for them. I see it so clearly now, almost twenty years later. At the time I couldn't believe that I had been so stupid! How could I let myself get into a situation like this?

I had been saving money from three jobs to go on a trip overseas on a tour with my choir. He cleaned out my bank account. Everything was gone. We broke up, but he never really left me alone.

I started saving again and managed to scrimp and save enough to still go on the trip, and to go on my own backpacking adventure after our tour ended. He invited me over to explain how he would pay me back for what he took, (even what he had stolen from my parents that I wasn't aware of at the time), and I foolishly went. His "plan" basically amounted to fraud, and when I refused to participate it got physical and he stole my wallet and coerced my new pin number for my new bank card from me.

I left in a daze, probably with a concussion, wandered home through a rough area of town without even a quarter to call for help. He emptied my bank account a second time.

I ended up making a police report. It couldn't go anywhere without corroboration, and he moved around too much to be served with a no-contact order, but it's there, on my record forever. When I went in to speak to the police, with my parents by my side, the douchebag officer behind the desk looked over at my stepdad and said, "This is always so hard on the dads, eh?" My stepdad looked him directly in the eye and said "I've only known about this for an hour. She has been dealing with it, alone, for a year. I think this is hardest on her!" We asked for a different officer to take my statement.

When I gave the new officer his name and she typed it into the system, she turned the screen towards me and said, "Is this him?"

My stomach dropped. There on the screen was his mugshot. A motherfucking MUGSHOT, along with a list of complaints and crimes that went on for several pages.

The world stopped. I felt sick. He had groomed me. He had zeroed in on me, and told me I was so special, so beautiful...

and then used me, taken my innocence in more ways than one, and also used me to swindle my friends and family. He was so very charming at first; everyone thought so. You just never know.

Every few years he would find me and send me a message, asking me to meet with him, or to forgive him, saying I looked good. The last one of those was a few years ago. I hope it was the last.

I wish I could say that that was the last abusive relationship that I got myself into. Unfortunately, that's not the case, and it took a couple of years, but I eventually left for good, and it also feels like a completely different life. I look around at my life now and can't even believe how lucky I am.

The thing is, I had the support of my family and friends, and I was lucky enough to find my way into a few other relationships that showed me what love truly is. I wish the same for everyone who's been in an abusive situation.

Look how far I've come. Whenever I fear that I just can't go on, or that I just don't have any strength left, I remember how much worse it has been, how much worse it still is for so many. *Don't be silly, Wenna,* I tell myself, *of course you can do this. Look at what you've already survived.*

When you work out and build muscle, you're actually creating micro-tears in your tissues that then heal, grow, and get stronger. When you break a bone, the spot where it knits back together is stronger than the rest of it. I think people can be like that. It's hard not to let these experiences keep pulling you back down, but if you can remain flexible and let yourself heal, you can be stronger than ever before. I have to remember that.

I hope we have a son, so that we can teach him about respect, consent, how to love, and to be loved.

I really hope we have a daughter, so that I can help her learn how strong she can be. And that whole thing about respect, consent, loving and being loved.

Self-Love...
No, Not That Kind.

My relationship with my body has always been tumultuous at best. I was raised in ballet from the age of five, had some questionable taste in men for a few years, plus, you know, life as a North American surrounded by constant media has an impact, so my body image has always been delicate. Unfortunately, this is something that pretty much everyone experiences, and it's good to see that body positivity is something that's becoming more mainstream.

In the past several years I've gotten addicted to the gym, I try to eat well, and with the love of my partner and friends, I am respecting just how much my body can do. I have tried to foster a loving relationship with it. I may not be able to fit into that killer outfit without feeling like an overstuffed sausage, but I can dance, walk, jump, and lift substantial weight without hurting myself. Push-ups and planks no longer terrify me, so I'm rather proud of that. Burpees...burpees will always suck. I don't care who you are. If you say they're fine— YOU LYIN'! But I digress.

With infertility, though, it was hard not to feel like my body had betrayed me. Like "I've gotten healthy and strong, and helped you to do so much more than you've ever been able to do before. Can't you do this one thing for me? Please?" Body doesn't answer. Body sips its fancy coffee and ignores me, like a petulant teenager being asked to mow the lawn.

I have had issues looking in the mirror before and finding myself too ugly for words (those abusive relationships leave deeper marks than just physical). Now I experienced the surreal feeling of being okay with, even liking, the image of myself in the mirror and being proud of the work

I had done, muscles I had toned, and the strength I had gained, while simultaneously being disgusted with my body for being barren.

A couple of friends of mine had gone to get boudoir shots done with this incredible photographer who specializes in making ladies of all shapes, sizes, and abilities feel beautiful and sexy. Valued. I hemmed and hawed about it for a year or two, and then decided to go myself. Kyle had always wanted me to do this, for me to see myself as he sees me, and to appreciate myself more. So in 2017, the year of "Fuck it! See what happens!" I went for my initial consult and booked the shoot. I then began to panic. As soon as I got home, I started to wonder what the hell I had just signed myself up for. After the year of financial acrobatics we had just been through, why was I spending so much money on PHOTOS?! Of me?! Randomly?! I called a friend who had had them done, (smokin', btw), and mentioned the small panic attack I was experiencing. She said many things. The thing I remember the most was her asking why I didn't feel that investing in myself was worth it. Why indeed? That changed my mindset almost instantly.

So. I went for my photo shoot.

Now, I have a background in theatre. I've been naked on stage. Hell, I've done nude choreography while covered in paint and wearing a gas mask (performance art is a hell of a thing, folks). But that wasn't ME—that was a character I put on. I've also changed in front of rooms full of people and been a happy, naked hippie running around with my happy, naked hippie friends in my teens and early twenties. This felt entirely different, and I wasn't completely sure that I wouldn't barf in front of the camera. Nothing says "sexy" like a lady in lingerie losing her lunch on film, ami-right? This was ME. There was nowhere to run, and I had to let myself be vulnerable. Once I got my makeup and hair done and we started shooting, the photographer immediately set me at ease. When she mentioned that I took direction well, and I told her that I used to be an actor, her eyes lit up and she got very excited, saying "Oh, THIS is gonna be fun!"

It really was. Every now and then I had a "Holy shit, I'm naked in front of a stranger while she takes pictures of me" moment in my head, but I shook it off and powered through. Ultimately, I'm glad I went. I left feeling strong and proud of myself, and the photos turned out beautifully. No, they will not be shared. They are a gift to myself and to Kyle.

Kyle went with me for "the reveal" and really enjoyed that the photographer seemed to echo things he tells me all the time. She told me to catch myself if I wanted to zero in on parts of my body that I hate, because no one else notices them. She said that I should look at the photos as if I were looking at someone else, because I would NEVER say the things I would say to/about myself to another woman—and she's absolutely right. Kyle was vibrating with satisfaction, as he tells me things like that ALL THE TIME. He always says to me: "if you had a daughter, would you let her see you treat yourself this way?"

At the very least, it was something that made me nervous, and I did it. It also helped me to love myself a bit more, so it was money well spent. We all have hang-ups about our bodies, whether it's love handles that we're not big fans of, or something more internal, like a disability (or inability to conceive a child, for example). I am endeavouring to appreciate and love all of the things that I CAN do, and that I AM proud of. It sounds cliché, and like something Oprah would preach, but we really do have to figure out how to love ourselves more. The whole world would be a better place, with less anger and pain, if we could just love more in general.

In continuing with this journey to self-love, I found a group of women at a yoga/support group for women who lost children or are struggling with infertility. We met in the instructor's home about every two weeks or so, and after a yoga class focused on restorative and "fertility inducing" poses, the eight of us sat around her table having tea and sharing stories about ourselves and our struggles. It's not a "misery loves company" type situation, it's just, once again, nice to feel justified in my anger, sadness, and frustration. Hearing other women share stories about how much this fertility doctor sucked, how much that hormone treatment messed them up, how expensive treatments are, how brutal infertility could be on a marriage, and how it affected their body image felt like a weight was being lifted, as if these other women were helping me carry it.

The morning of my first class with these women was great. I left on a cloud, feeling thankful, proud, and peaceful. That night I went to a stagette for a friend of mine.

All of us ladies met in the privately reserved lounge of a restaurant, and then went in for dinner. It was nice. Despite barely knowing these women, and my friend (the bride) being at a different table, I was feeling welcomed and enjoying a glass of wine and some small talk. Then I realized that I had inadvertently sat at THE WRONG table; at our table of six, two of the women were pregnant. So guess what we were going to talk about! In my head, as I smiled and sat down, I thought "Oh good. This will be fun." We did talk about kids, kids names, pregnancy, among other things. Then we played a game in which there is a giant ball of plastic wrap with prizes lodged inside. The grand prize in the middle of this environmental disaster was a pregnancy test for the bride. Everyone laughed, as it was a lot of fun, and a funny joke for when the bride and groom start trying for a kid. I figured it was a good time for me to leave. While these ladies were a lot of fun and doing their best to include me, it was harshing my buzz from earlier in the day when I'd been feeling better about things. I wanted to get back to that place instead of allowing negativity back in, so I said my goodbyes, paid my bill, and went home to snuggles with Kyle and our dog.

It is important for me to keep remembering that even if I'm feeling lonely, I HAVE been at peace with things and I WILL be again. I have a group who understands what I'm feeling and is going through it with me. I have friends and family who love me, I'm married to my best friend, and I have a pretty great life. I just need to give myself permission to remove myself from situations that aren't good for me. It's okay to fluctuate emotionally on this roller coaster, I just have to remember how to bring myself back. And love myself.

Part
5

An Offer We Couldn't Refuse

Yet again, just when we thought we were at the end of the road, something happened to set us on another path and we decided to look into the possibility of conceiving through in vitro fertilization. This is a very expensive (and invasive!) process, one that we had never considered because there was no way we could afford it.

But then Kyle's parents offered to help pay for a round of IVF for us. By which I mean cover the majority of it. Whoa. Once I regained mental capacity and we talked and thought and talked and thought some more about it, Kyle and I decided that it was too good of an opportunity to pass up.

If it failed, then that would hurt but at least I would have tried. I needed to keep trying to be a mom, and if it didn't work out, and the whole process sucked, then at least it was only temporary. I needed to remember that.

But just how far down the rabbit hole were we willing to go? Would I fully commit? Jump in with both feet? Could I stay pragmatic and avoid getting heartbroken if it didn't work? It wasn't my money, so I felt extra pressure—completely self-imposed, as my in-laws would absolutely NEVER make us feel bad for "wasting their money" on a failed attempt. I'm just an expert at putting undue pressure on myself.

But you know, when you're good at something...

In the end we figured we would try it, but only once. After five years of watching friends try multiple times only to have it not work and come crashing down both emotionally and financially, the thought of plugging up to $60,000 into a VLT machine that has less than favourable odds of ever hitting the jackpot wasn't so appealing. If it didn't work out then at least we'd know that we'd tried everything, and maybe (MAYBE) it would be easier to close the door on that part of our plan and our lives and move forward with the plan of being DINKs and spoiling our family and friends' kids.

So, we were in our new home, all unpacked, and our adoption file renewed. We had jumped through about a million hoops with doctors and referrals; and we did some facting and figuring about where to undergo this process. I'd been to the fertility clinic in Winnipeg, but I also had several friends who had done IVF in other provinces or the US. We went back and forth for a while about the possibility of better clinics in other provinces, but in the end, it was way more money and WAY more time. Plus, there would be added cost of the flights there and back repeatedly, for simple appointments like taking my temperature, that I'd also have to take time off work for. Those same appointments here would only take an hour or two out of my day before sending me on my merry way. Okay, probably not merry, especially with rage-inducing hormones coursing through my veins and my glass of wine taken away, but I digress.

Long story short—we would be attempting this next journey here at home. Our first official appointment to get the process started was booked. And I was dangerously close to that feeling of hope again.

Over the last few years, I'd built up a rather comfy wall of emotional safety around myself. I (sometimes rather effectively) convinced myself that I didn't actually want kids anyway. They're expensive, and I'll miss sleep and being selfish, and I work too much anyway, and the world is overpopulated and yada yada yada. For the most part this wall kept me safe and happy. There was no more pain behind the numb wall of illusion.

Except then fourteen more pregnancy announcements pop up at once and I'd dissolve into tears and remember that I really DID want this. Goddammit.

We lived next to a splash pad, and I couldn't help but imagine taking my child to join the other happily squeeing kid frenzy. I love our guest room but couldn't help picturing it as a nursery. Again. This was dangerous territory.

How was I supposed to feel? If we were going to try this—REALLY try this, I felt like I should probably allow myself to be hopeful again. What if all of those *Secret* books are true? What if my negative attitude infects my life more than I thought it could? Didn't I owe it to us to jump in with both feet and be fully on board? Probably, but HOLY SHIT IS THAT EVER SCARY AND I MISS MY SAFE WALL OF PROTECTION.

Welp! Here we go again!

Before trying IVF, our doctor recommended that we try a few rounds of IUI (intrauterine insemination, so basically a glorified turkey baster with a tonne of hormone treatments and clinical procedures to help) because:

1. IVF is hella expensive ($24,000 or more, versus $1500 + donor sperm for each round of IUI),
2. IVF takes a LOT of time and appointments, and
3. IVF is brutal. The hormone treatments, the constant needles, the pain and discomfort of using meds and hormones, and some incredibly painful procedures… all just ducky.

Our doctor had explained to us how unlikely getting pregnant with Kyle's sperm might be, so we decided to move forward with donor sperm. It's exhausting and bureaucratic, and we had to find out if my genetics would resist or attack certain types of sperm, but it turned out that I could have any donor sperm I wanted.

Before we could get access to the donor catalogue, however, we had to go for mandatory counselling. Hoop. Jumping. Expert level.

Once we were in that appointment, the counsellor asked us about our journey with infertility so far. After I told her to buckle up, and Kyle filled her in on our saga, and her eyes returned to a normal size, she mentioned our inner "cup." People only have a finite amount of space inside them (a cup, if you will) for stress and negative emotions to pile up before it overflows. If you stub your toe and burst into tears, it likely has more to do with your cup being full than the actual toe-stubbage. So it's important to find ways to drain your cup on a regular basis, especially when undergoing stressful things like…oh, I don't know…five years of the adoption and infertility processes while also having a super stressful job (I'm spitballing here). Despite my usual cup-draining activities of gym classes, attempts at meditation etc., it appears that our cups weren't completely drained.

One day Kyle and I decided to use a gift certificate to go and see a feel-good movie. The movie hadn't even started yet and I was in tears. Those freaking movie trailers, man! First up, we had *Dumbo*. Now, I am still so deeply affected by Disney's *Dumbo* from when I was a kid, that I can't handle it even now—that poor, scared little guy—and the scene where his mom's trunk comforts him through the bars of her cage?! COME ON! This new Tim Burton version looked even more heart-wrenching, so I was a mess.

Then, in a double-whammy, we had the trailer for the new *Dog's Purpose* film. What if your dog dies and is reincarnated in another dog and keeps finding you and your family over and over again? I was sobbing. Which happens with me sometimes, but this was a bit much. I looked over at Kyle to accept his usual light-hearted mockery of my snot-and-tears situation and he was wiping away his own tears! I was stunned.

He is a good man, with plenty of feelings, but he's not so much with the showing of these feelings. I'd seen him cry only four times in the twelve years I'd known him. He got misty at our wedding but didn't shed a tear. He cried when he met his biological family (privately, with me).

He cried when his Granny died, and he cried with me when we lost our adopted boy. All pretty serious stuff.

Welp! Now we can add "*Dumbo* trailer" to the list. I guess his cup was full!

We laughed about it all the way home from the movie.

"Hey Kyle, when's the last time you cried?"

"Well, the answer used to be when we lost a child, but HEY, have you seen that new *Dumbo* trailer?"

My cup seems to spend most of its time approaching fullness, but it's oddly nice to know that he wasn't immune to the stress either. He turned to me and asked, "Is this how you live?! HOW?!"

Hahahahahahahaha!!!! Yes. Yes, it is.

The Moment When Everything Changed

When I was a kid, I loved my mom and brother. I had some friends but wasn't hugely popular. My dad, though, my dad was my world. He got me. He called me "weird and wonderful" and always made me feel like the prettiest and coolest girl in the room—other than mom, of course. The fact that I may have been the ONLY girl in the room at the time is irrelevant. He said repeatedly that he couldn't wait to see us grow up and have kids of our own; that he was excited to see the kind of mother that I'd become. He was funny and creative and strict when he needed to be (or when he'd let me get away with way too much crap and the brattiness got out of hand). And even though he was "that" teacher—the one who made huge differences in his students' lives and was constantly working or marking at the dining room table—he always made time for me. We were peas in a pod.

Then, when I was just about to turn fourteen, my whole world changed. We had all gone to my baby cousin's christening that morning, and then that afternoon I was at home doing homework and nursing a cold, mom was taking a nap upstairs and my big brother, William, was out with his girlfriend while Dad was performing with his dance troupe in a big park in our city. It was a beautiful fall day, and the weather couldn't have been nicer for an outdoor performance.

I was surrounded by Kleenex and snack wrappers, when suddenly there were cops knocking on the door. Our little dog was losing his shit, so I had to run upstairs to wake mom up to see what the hell was going on. The apologetic park police officers informed us that my dad had had "an episode" and had been taken to the hospital. What the hell does "an episode" mean? We kept asking, but the cops just said that we needed to come with them and get hold of William to have him meet us there.

When we got to the hospital, the doctor and some of the Morris Men from the dance troupe were waiting to fill us in. Between dances, my dad had gone into ventricular fibrillation, sank down onto his knees while clutching his heart, had said "Oh my, this is not good" and then gone rigid. His buddies had done CPR on him for twenty minutes until the ambulance arrived, and the paramedics had gotten his heart going again with a shot of adrenaline and taken him to the hospital, but he was still unconscious.

We went in to see him and he looked...weird. His colour was wrong, and he looked so small. This man who was larger than life really wasn't a very big guy, and I had never really noticed it until that moment. He had all sorts of tubes and things connected to him to help him breathe, and I was afraid to touch him, but we talked to him and held his hand. It was so surreal, and we were all on autopilot. Mom sent me home with my grandma that night, and I remember being sent to school at some point, maybe two days later. I protested and said I needed to stay at the hospital but was overruled and told that if anything big happened, they'd send Will to come and pull me out of class.

Well, needless to say, school sucked; but the upside was that my less-than-nice classmates had heard the news and were nicer to me that day. To a thirteen- almost-fourteen-year-old, that was oddly satisfying. Will picked me up at the end of the day and took me to the hospital. I had wanted to swing home first to get a book of stories that Dad had always read to me so that I could read to him, but Will said that we had to get back. I swear I heard "Dun DUN DUUUUUNNNNNN" in my head, but tried to shrug it off, because OF COURSE Dad was going to be fine. Dad was the guy who scared monsters away and made everything feel safe. He was my best friend—obviously he would be fine, albeit probably embarrassed about the big fuss.

Well, apparently not. When we got back to the hospital, I was informed that even though they had gotten his heart going again, his brain had just been without oxygen for too long. Dad was in a coma and was never going to wake up.

I don't remember much about what happened next. I remember flashes of the family room in the hospital and being brought Arby's a lot (there was one close to the hospital), and a strawberry milkshake. I remember my aunts flying in from Alberta—one a very experienced nurse, and the other a fancypants pathologist with a good reputation. I remember being amused because my aunt finally got our doctor to act like a human being. Doctor McD-bag had been less than helpful at first; his ego must have made it difficult to fit through the door. He talked down to us (including to my mom) like we couldn't possibly understand what was happening, not being doctors ourselves, so my aunt simply barged into the doctor's area, gave her name and credentials, and demanded to be told what was happening with her brother. She also had a doctor called in that she had gone to school with. It was awesome.

The decision was made that he would never want to live... well, not really live, exist like this. We had to pull the plug and take him off of life support. We had to let him go.

We still pretty much lived at the hospital, visiting his bedside whenever we could. He was always a huge music lover, so I brought my Walkman from home.

I figured that this would reach him no matter how far away he was and would be a distraction from the beeping and other crappy hospital noises. We kept having to leave the room though, so that the nurses could vacuum the fluid off of his lungs, not so much for him (they said he no longer felt pain) but for us, because it sounded awful and incredibly painful. I'll never forget it. The sounds and smells of death are intense.

Whenever we got home, we would find deliveries of cards, flowers, baking and casseroles from people who knew us, or simply had known and loved my dad. It was super thought-ful, and also handy—our chest freezer in the basement was packed full, and we didn't have to cook for a month. One time, Will and I were home alone and answered the door to find a woman holding some sort of rich-looking cake. She said that she had known Dad ages ago (she had actually been one of his students, once upon a time), and was so sorry to hear that he was in hospital. She asked how he was doing, and when we told her that he had been taken off life support and it was only a matter of time, she looked like she had been shot. This was the kind of impression my dad made on people—I had no idea who this woman was, but she was so affected by Dad's death that I was concerned for her safety while she was driving away.

One night, my aunt and uncle had us all over for dinner to get a break from the hospital. It was really nice to all be together, and there were a lot of tears and laughs that night. So, of course, Dad chose that as his exit moment. Rude. No one was there, and that still haunts me, but I think he probably did it on purpose somehow. I think he wanted us all to be together and supporting each other while he slipped out the back door.

I remember being in the room with him, while mom went to make arrangements with the doctors and nurses with William for support. I remember putting my head on his chest, like I had so many times before when we used to snuggle when I was little. I remember that he was cold, with no heartbeat. I had listened to the strong and comforting lub-dub in his chest so many times as a kid, I remember it being really weird and silent. The room smelled like death—the pungent aroma of a human body shutting down. I remember my brother wanting to see Dad's eyes one last time, so my aunt went to move the ice pack that was over his eyes (to keep his cornea cold for donation) and opened his eyes with delicate fingers, and I turned away. I had already heard and smelled his death; I didn't want to see his eyes without their usual life and sparkle. Several months later, we got a letter from the woman who had gotten Dad's cornea. She was so sorry for our loss, but so grateful, and hoped that we found some solace in knowing that because of his donation—she could see. That was pretty special.

So, my fourteenth birthday wasn't great. Two weeks into grade nine in a new school—high school—and then everything changed at once. Dad's funeral was the day before my birthday. We were once again reminded of the impact he had had on so many people. The service was at our church, and the building was packed. When I say the building, I mean the whole building: the sanctuary, the stairs, the basement hall, and folks were even lined up outside and down the street like they were waiting for concert tickets. Those that couldn't make it into the building simply stood for the length of the service, and then dissipated. We were deeply touched.

My sense of safety and innocence after that was more or less in shambles, which was surprisingly liberating. I had always been a nerd; not with the "in crowd." I was into choir and theatre and *Star Trek* (Dad had raised us on *Star Trek*). I never had the right outfits, or the right tight little body to go in the right outfits. I had glasses and a lazy eye, and a few too many pounds. I was always so concerned with what other people thought, then suddenly I was faced with the reality that life is short, so why should I give a flying fuck what the popular kids thought of me.

I was angry and pretending to be confident during the day, finally standing up to some asshats in my school, but spending my nights battling insomnia, wrapped in a huge scarf my dad used to wear. He used to like *Dr. Who*, and Tom Baker in particular, so my aunt had crocheted him a really long patchwork scarf of his own—it made for several wraps around my shoulders, and I found it really comforting for a time. Plus, it smelled like Dad had smelled before going into the hospital. Safe.

Shopping for Sperm

A fter our mandatory counselling where we learned about our "inner cups," we also learned that we could've been shopping for sperm for ages. There were two online banks to choose from, with a plethora of opportunies to feel like a horrible person. The selection was…plentiful. So much so that we quickly got overwhelmed and needed to narrow the search parameters, which could be done by race, interests/ hobbies, medical information, education level, and so on. We had our adoption file wide open to all races, ages etc., but sifting through literally thousands of sperm donors was just too much. We felt a bit ruthless as we picked and chose who to consider, like the fussiest Tinder date ever.

The next thing to consider was which bank to go with. One provided a TONNE of info: the donor's photos, medical history, family medical history, allergies etc. The other was more like a vaguely anonymous dating profile: "Donor #1234 enjoys hiking, yoga, reading, playing chess, and singing. He has kind eyes and our staff finds him attractive."

We opted for the latter. The profile described someone that we'd imagine and hope for our kid to be. We didn't want to know too much about the donor. If we saw photos of the sperm donor, then we'd see him in our kid. Better that our kid is just our kid. We knew that they were screened heavily, or they wouldn't be allowed to donate, so we weren't too concerned about getting an entire medical profile. We had to go with what felt right, and also just make a damn decision, because tick-tock, and also it got overwhelming really quickly with all of the options. There is a LOT of frozen sperm out there! Holy hell.

I'll try to spare you most of the super gritty details about the process, but I will say that I had to go back on Letrozole again. The testosterone-fuelled rages that consumed me last time didn't happen this time; maybe because I was only required to be on it for five days. Or maybe because they didn't discuss dosage with me AT ALL, so I was only on a third of what I was supposed to be on. The most I had was some dizziness and nausea which was manageable. I had to monitor my cycle and go for another internal ultrasound to see how my follicles were doing. Ultrasound day? This is a thing, I guess. They said to be there at 7:30 a.m., and that it was first come first served. They don't even open until 8:00, so when we arrived before 7:00, I felt pretty good—until the elevator doors opened on a hallway full of women camped out, looking miserable, waiting. Good. Great. Grand.

My ultrasound said I had two "large" follicles, so…good then. Then they handed me an ovulation test kit and sent me on my way.

Ovulation tests are fussy. I had to test at a certain time of day without diluting myself with too much water, and I was having trouble working it around my schedule, so I took it to the gym. Cuz hanging out in a public gym bathroom, waiting in a stall while trying not to lean on any surfaces because EWW, seemed like a good idea, I guess. With women outside of the stall probably wondering what I was doing. Fun times! Anyway, I finally got my "happy face" on the test and called the clinic to book my insemination for the next day.

IUI

As expected, my sleep was somewhat fitful the night before. Gotta love those ever helpful four a.m. thoughts. What will it be like? Is it going to hurt? Dude, tomorrow I'm going to let a stranger put a different stranger's semen inside me. What does the plunger/ turkey baster thingie look like? Is it like a crazy straw? WHAT IF IT'S A CRAZY STRAW?!

Luckily, it was during spring break, so Kyle was off work and able to come with me. On the drive there, we were talking about how the success rate for IUI goes up each time you do it with no explanation as to why. First time has a success rate of about 10-15% (maybe a bit less because of my "advanced age"). Second time it's more like 10-30%, and some studies show an efficacy of about 50% by the sixth time. (SIXTH MF TIME?! Oh God. Please, no.)

Kyle had his own theories about the cumulative success rate. Which were hilarious:

> First try, my eggs are all:
> "Eeeeeewwww! It's all sticky! Get it OFF! Gross! Blech! Nasty!"
> But by the sixth try:
> "Oh yeah! This stuff! I LOVE this stuff! Give it! Roll around in it! YEAH!"

Kyle was nervous in his own way, which oddly made me feel much better…mostly. Kyle shows his nerves sometimes by being funny or awkward (yet another reason that he's a good match for me). Lean into it, I guess! He decided that he wanted to stare me in the eye during the insemination, so that it wouldn't be so weird knowing that it was some stranger's sperm. This did NOT work, but it did make me giggle. Which made things harder for the nurse who was trying to do her job between the stirrups. She was lovely though, and actually thought that our odd humour was sweet.

Turns out my insides are apparently configured differently, so she had to rearrange some things to make the insemination work—which felt GREAT, lemme just say. She also had to keep removing the plunger straw thingie to bend it this way and then that way INTO A CRAZY STRAW SHAPE to get it to work for me.

I knew it.

After it was all done, I hung out on the table/bed for about ten minutes to let gravity help a bit while we chatted, and the nurse handed me a prescription for yet another type of hormone to be taken twice a day for twenty days (ten weeks if I ended up pregnant) to make me more "sticky" inside. She told me to go back to my day and try to relax, but my phone exploded with about twenty-five texts and calls from a panicky client, so off I went with fantastic cramps, wondering if I had just been impregnated.

This whole hope thing. I've talked about it many times, but it's a hell of a thing. We knew the odds, but how do you not hope when you're putting yourself through so much. You HAVE to believe that it is all for a good reason. I found myself hoping like I hadn't in years. My brain was telling me not to get excited, but the whole while the rest of me was having little conversations with my belly. "Are you in there, little one? Just hold on tight. Please."

It was also super hard not to get excited because—FUN FACT—the sticky hormones give many of the side effects of early pregnancy. They should really warn you, no? For two and a half weeks I felt almost constant nausea, cramping, and more exhaustion than I've ever experienced. Making it through the day with my eyes open without a nap was brutal.... so I must be pregnant, yes? Brain—"No. The likelihood of pregnancy is extremely slim. Calm down." Body—"PREGNANT! WE ARE PREGNANT HERE, FOLKS!" Heart—swells with hope, then spasms and remembers all of the let-downs over the last several years with this, then swells again, then crashes etc.

At any rate, the day finally came to go and give my blood test to see if it had worked. I went in the morning and waited by my phone for the rest of the day to hear. I couldn't call the clinic myself. They would call and leave me a message, I'd call and leave my own message, and back and forth it went, but with test results—they couldn't leave a message. I also have an old house, so sometimes my phone would just notify me that I had a missed call and voicemail without ever actually ringing. This was a PERFECT time to have this happen. Repeatedly. Eventually I managed to catch a nurse as they were leaving the clinic for the day, and she informed me that I was not pregnant.

Bad day. Send gifs.

Over the next few months, we went through a few failed rounds of IUI. There were adventures with wrong dosages of hormones, missed ovulation windows, many, many early mornings of getting in line to sit down the hallway outside the clinic in a first-come-first-served fashion for ultrasounds and blood tests, like the line-ups for the worst black

Friday sale ever. I'd heard of what's called a "trigger shot," and while I was hoping to avoid having to inject hormones into my stomach to stimulate ovulation, I wasn't so lucky. So that's a new experience I can add to my witty dinner conversations.

Hormones are incredibly powerful little a-holes. The doctors don't tell you much about what to expect, or about the side-effects.. They may not warn you about the acne, nausea, exhaustion, severe depression, or rapid mental health decline. They may mention some of the physiological effects, like tender breasts or weight fluctuation, but none of the mental or emotional ones. I got to experience all of these effects! Full-serve hormonal experience, please! Everything hurt, I gained weight, got acne like I hadn't had since I was a teenager, I was nauseous and beyond exhausted all of the time, and my mental health felt like I was hanging on by the tiniest of threads.

That year I felt like I was constantly veering towards the negative side of the road. I was quick to anger, snippier, and generally someone who said or thought something and then wondered why the hell I said or did THAT. Was it the hormones? (Quite possibly, they do really affect me). Was it the roller coaster of hope and then despair finally wearing me down? Was it just something that was happening for now, and I would get back to myself over time?

I found myself worrying more and more about how this was all changing me. We are who we are in large part because of the storms that we weather. But was it changing me into someone I no longer liked?

Pain was just the recurring background pattern in our lives, like bad wallpaper that you can't quite ignore successfully. We know that chronic pain changes people. Does that include emotional pain? Are those changes permanent?

We chose to take a break and took a trip to Scotland and Ireland for a couple of weeks. It was amazing, it was wonderful, it was exhausting, and it was hella expensive, but we had so many joyful moments that were a welcome change. We had laughs, awesome food, shitty food, lovely scotches and beers, adventures, misadventures, oopsies, and great chats with friends. Being reminded that there was a whole world out there outside of our struggles did help. We even got matching tattoos in Ireland in Ogham (ancient Irish script) that says "Sonas," which means happiness. Now whenever we're sad, we can remember that we always have happiness with us and can make the choice to follow it. Because it can be a choice sometimes; I need to choose to be happy. In theory.

When we returned, I'd start the IUI process again, and if that didn't work, we figured we should probably try IVF. I didn't want to, and it would be hard—I was told that the side effects of the hormones were going to be so much worse, and the time commitment and emotional and mental fortitude required would be intense—but if we didn't try, we'd always wonder "what if."

In the meantime, my stepbrother and his fiancée were expecting a baby girl, and though we'd pulled back from them a bit to avoid the baby conversations and the ever-growing baby bump, they honoured us by choosing us to be their baby's godparents. This took some of the sting out of the growing possibility that we might simply never have a family of our own. At least we would be able to contribute to the raising of this kid, and maybe steal her away for the odd camping trip or something that we longed to take our own child on. It would also give us a good excuse to go to the splash pad by our house when it was a million degrees out, as going without a kid would probably seem odd and creepy.

I felt that I owed it to her, as well as my other nieces and nephew, to try to dig myself out of this hole. I needed to be me again, or at least try to shake some of the dust off and see the light.

For six years (our entire marriage) we'd been trying to start a family: we'd spent five years on the adoption "list," experienced a failed adoption, gone through multiple attempts at pregnancy including all of the gross, expensive, painful, and ridiculous methods that should surely work (because they did for so-and-so), and the insemination attempts with donor sperm. The past year had been brutal. The roller coaster, constant doctor's appointments, dietary changes, physical changes, and hormone manipulation that went along with the IUI attempts took a huge toll. We decided that the third IUI attempt would be our last. After that we would consider IVF, but IUI was going to work, we told ourselves, so it didn't matter.

This last attempt was the worst of all. Even knowing by now that the hormones would make me feel exhausted, nauseous, incredibly depressed, and that I'd gain weight, hurt all over, and all of the things that indicate pregnancy, this time it really felt real. This time we were pretty positive that the universe had FINALLY smiled on us, and that my repeated, incredibly vivid dreams that I was carrying a baby girl who would be healthy and perfect were coming true.

I spent three weeks agonizing, waiting, and feeling like general garbage, but being okay with it because it clearly meant I was pregnant, and then went early in the morning to have my blood tested. Then I waited all the long day for my test results.

Nada.

When I finally did get the call with my test results, I was opening up a show home for a five-hour open house. I couldn't fall apart. I had to call Kyle and give him the news over the phone and still hold my shit together. I had work to do, and people (and their freakishly adorable babies, because of course they had to come to my show home at that moment) to charm and smile at.

So, hah! Look, Ma, I DO use my theatre degree!

The dissolution of everything that I am and ever was happened in the car on the way home, and then again when Kyle greeted me in tears at the door. It's not okay. The realization that I'd never be called Mom hit me like a ton of bricks. I like to think I'd be a great mom, and I KNOW Kyle would be an incredible dad, and it's just not fucking fair.

We had yet to go and talk to our doc about IVF, but we had no more faith, and our spirits were broken. I had nothing left. IVF is expensive, and painful, and even more invasive and exhausting, and also doesn't have the greatest success rate. Why the fuck would we put ourselves through this anymore? Would it be better in the long run to start our mourning process and finally move forward with our lives, after six years of this bullshit? Or was it worth it to try this one last thing on the off chance that we might finally get some luck? How long does it take? Are we signing on for another two years of hell? These are all things that we would inquire about, but we weren't hopeful. A reader of my blog reached out, telling me that she was training for her first marathon—a crazy hard one up a mountain—because it was more appealing than more IUI or IVF attempts. This shit blows. It's so bad that people prefer RUNNING UP A MOUNTAIN to subjecting themselves to it.

Doctors and Science and Delays, Oh My!

As we got ready to try IVF and ICSI treatments, we tried to prepare for future craziness with hormones, because this was likely going to be so much worse. On the bright side, my doctor told me that I'd be too distracted by the painful, gross, and uncomfortable things my body would be going through to be as affected by the depression and despair I experienced with IUI.

We created a little sanctuary in our house that would remind me of trips, good times, and a world outside of infertility. I downloaded some meditation apps geared towards IVF victims... er... patients and bought a yoga membership that I could use when I was no longer able to go to my workouts.

We went to mandatory therapy again, but it was basically the exact appointment we had had the previous time for IUI, so we just chatted. Going before the IVF process begins for a "brace yourself—this is really going to suck" appointment is valuable and all, but finding therapy to help you through the months of treatments would be more helpful.

I called around to several places to try to find a therapist for this journey, but it seemed that no one was taking new patients, and the waiting list for therapy covered by Health Canada is at least six months long. I hoped that the therapist appointment and the wonderful support network that we had would be enough to help me stay grounded.

I was terrified, nervous, and not at all looking forward to the process, but I was a bit excited to see a light at the end of the tunnel. After this process, we would either have a child or we wouldn't. If we didn't, it would be sad, but we would finally be able to start to move on.

Part

6

Is the Universe Trying to Tell Me Something?

IVF is complicated; of course it is. For basic IVF, doctors fill a petri dish already containing an egg with sperm, to facilitate the natural fertilization process, or shorten the length of the swim the sperm have to make. I assume they turn down the lights, crank up the Barry White, leave for a while and hope for the best, but I'm not a doctor. For ICSI (intracytoplasmic sperm injection—what we were going to have to do), the doctors take sperm and inject it into an egg to grow in a petri dish. They inject one single sperm to one single egg, depending on how many eggs they can grow and retrieve. Then if the embryos survive for five days, they are implanted (one at a time) into the uterus with hormonal help, and everyone hopes for the best. That said, Kyle and I do seem to have a knack for making things more ridiculous than usual (see our adoption misadventures).

Three times we went to our very poorly run local fertility clinic to "start" the IVF process. Get things rolling. Get me knocked up. Tick tock, people! Instead of beginning things, however, we were informed that Kyle has a rare genetic disorder that affects his Y-chromosome. (I always knew he was special and unique!) It is the reason for his low sperm count. In fact, his little dudes are an irregular shape as well, so they wouldn't be able to impregnate anyone in the natural way. It also lowers our chances of IVF being successful. This was a huge blow, especially to Kyle, who felt like he's "ruined my life," which is, of course, absolutely untrue. I understand the feeling though, as it's how I felt when we thought it was my body being uncooperative for those years.

Kyle's condition is passed down from father to son and gets more severe with each generation, so his biological father would've had it as well, but was obviously still able to have children. Kyle can still produce *some* sperm, but they're spherical instead of tadpole shaped (he's taken to calling them his little army of pellets) and can't survive the natural impregnating process. If Kyle has a son, he won't produce sperm at all. Ever. Baby boy may also have other congenital defects, but because this condition is rare, the research is new, and since studies on babies and pregnant women can't be done ethically (duh) there are a shit tonne of unknowns. On the other hand, if we had a girl, she should be fine, as it's only the Y-chromosome that is affected.

Our doctor suggested that it might be possible to take a two-pronged approach. For example, if I could drop ten eggs, they could inject five of them with Kyle's pellet soldiers and five of them with donor sperm. That way he could watch how both petri dishes of embryos grow and decide which looked healthier, stronger, less likely to miscarry, and also which had more female embryos. But first he'd have to speak in front of a committee to ask permission to do this as using only female embryos raises a lot of ethical and human rights questions.

Damn did I ever appreciate simple choices like never before. What kind of coffee do I want? What do I want for lunch? What should I watch on Netflix?

Our feelings about all this were beyond complicated. What if we had a boy and, other than being infertile, he's completely healthy? What if it turns out that he doesn't care about having kids?

Do we just roll the dice and hope to have a girl or hope to have a boy who somehow doesn't mind being subjected to the agony of infertility KNOWINGLY by the two people who understand it most…because we are selfish and want a child so badly. And though we are still on the adoption list, who knows if we will get chosen again. Another alternative would be to only use donor sperm rather than Kyle's, as we had with IUI.

We were told to go see a geneticist for more definite answers, then go back to see our doc. The geneticist also took several calls to get hold of (as is tradition) only to find out that the waiting list is two years long. So we called our doc back (every day for almost two weeks; as is still tradition. FFS) and he was flabbergasted at the wait time. He said he would call a colleague and hopefully get more answers from him, and that we should call him back on Monday to book another appointment to hear what he found out and *finally start the process.* We then found out that "Monday" meant once again calling every day for another two weeks to make an appointment for the next month. *FFS once again.*

We went to our next appointment and were told that we would have to wait another five months for a specialist to come from Toronto. Apparently, this dude is the "God" of sperm retrieval—basically it's a bunch of syringes to the testicles (sounds like fun) to locate and retrieve sperm to study and hopefully to be able to use for IVF. So okay, cool. More waiting. I'll just sit over here getting older and wondering if they make a baby stroller with a walker attachment, or if I'll be that mom who gets mistaken for Grandma, and trying not to think about how my dad died young.

We were back in a holding pattern while waiting for specialists for our IVF adventure, but once we finally got going with this for real, I'd have to remind myself not to wallow for too long. It does nobody any good.

In the meantime, I spent several days crying and letting my brain take me into a negative spiral (hormones did not help). Horrible and unhelpful thoughts flew back and forth. Things like: Is the universe trying to tell us something? Like stop already, kids aren't for you! Or is it testing us to make sure that we are truly serious? Why don't other people get this many trip ups? They can just get pregnant without even wanting to. I felt like a petulant child whining about how "IT'S JUST NOT FAIR!!!"

My brain's newest adventure was getting me to wonder what my life *could've* been like if kids had never been on the agenda. I'd made just about every major decision in my life based on the idea of kids in my future. I've broken up with partners who didn't want "the life," with the house, the kids, the jobs etc. I lived the vagabond artist life for years, happily travelling and working and making music, theatre, and art while making ends meet with side jobs (as one does). I loved it. But as the years passed, I knew I would have to get a "real" job and find a serious partner who wanted the same things so that we could build a home and raise a family together.

I chose everything, EVERYTHING with the eventuality and possibility of kids. The last several cars I owned were four-door and had to accommodate a car seat and have storage for kid crap. I chose to stay in Canada instead of some of the amazing places that stole my heart and called to me because it's where I wanted to raise my family. I chose Kyle as my partner because…well, I fell head over heels for him and he's amazing in so many ways, but also because he is incredible with children, badly wants them too, and has a solid job and plan for the future. I chose my apartments and houses with kids in mind. I chose my job in part because it has a somewhat flexible schedule and seemed like it could work well with Kyle's schedule for childcare.

What would my life look like now if kids had never been on my radar? If I never thought I wanted them or knew that it probably wouldn't happen for me. Would I be an artist living in Europe somewhere? Would I have done well in theatre and film if I'd stuck it out? Would I still be travelling the world making music and theatre?

I mean, the grass is always greener, and in all likelihood I would probably be listening to my alternate-dimension scumbag brain, getting sick of living like a nomad and eating dinners out of a can, wondering what my life would look like in a loving marriage, with a cozy home in a cute community, with the car and dog and … pot roast dinners, I guess? It's all useless thinking, and I truly do love my life. And sometimes I was momentarily thankful that I wasn't a parent. Like that week I was struck down with the plague. Okay, it was a really bad cold, but I was SO HORRIBLY SICK, guys! Kyle said I got a man cold because that's how his colds always are. Alright, Kyle. Parents don't get days off. They can't just lie there and leak, ooze and moan and be miserable if they're sick—they have little humans to take care of. Pot roasts to make.

Brains are funny things. They are capable of amazing thoughts and creativity, they keep us breathing and walking and having motor functions etc., but they can also lead us down odd or dangerous paths if we're not careful. I'll speak for myself: I need to feel sad sometimes, especially if something traumatic is happening in my life, but I also need to remember to focus on things to be thankful for and live in the now, and it's amazing what that does sometimes. Cheesy, but true.

SUMMER OF MO

So. IVF. Wonderful opportunity, incredible gift, terrifying experience. I was trying to look at it as something that I GOT to do, rather than something that I HAD to go through. So…good luck with that…I say to myself.

Truly I thought that it would be a good exercise overall. Baby = Yay! IVF not working = sad but would give us the ability (in theory) to finally move on with a DINKWAD life (Dual Income No Kids With A Dog). Plus having my crutches like delicious wine, helpful CBD etc. taken away would force me to find other habits to get into—other ways to deal with stress. I'd get more serious about daily meditations. Do yoga more. I enjoyed both of these things, but it was easy for me to make excuses not to do them.

BUT! Until then…

SUMMER OF MO!!!

SUMMER OF MO: a hedonistic and somewhat selfish escape, because we'd been through a lot and I was willingly signing on for torture. Think "babymoon," but without the promise of a baby at the end of it.

Because the next several months could very well suck for me—being the automatic DD for my friends, with added hormones and stress, with no guarantees of success at the end—this summer was my excuse to eat, drink and do the things that I usually would have to waffle back and forth on.

"Hey Mo, would you like a glass of wine?"

"No, that's okay, I…. SUMMER OF MO!! YES PLEASE!"

"Wanna go in the hot tub?"

"I sure do! SUMMER OF MO!!"

"Sushi for dinner?"

"SUMMER...OF...MOOOOOOOO!!!"

You get the idea. This way of living or making snap decisions resulted in some experiences that I might not have otherwise had. Like getting drunk with my in-laws. By accident. I swear! Kyle's folks came for a visit that summer, and while we were having a fire out back one night, my father-in-law was in charge of pouring the scotches. He poured two fingers—but they were vertical fingers, not horizontal. We had some really great talks and giggles and got to say how thankful we really are for the IVF opportunity that they're giving us. While the next day kinda sucked for me, the chats that happened around that fire will be cherished memories for me forever. What I can remember of them, anyway.

Some other cool stuff I got to do that summer included things like Folkfest. I go every year and usually camp as well, but that year Kyle finally came along! It was wonderful. Five days of filthy camping, a ton of walking, lots of late-night giggles with dear friends, cold beer, SO much amazing music, good food, campfires, and my best friend/husband with me for all of it. Now when I tell stories about people wandering around in glow-y costumes, hippie fishing, speaking in "Yip yip yip, uh huh, uh huh" from *Sesame Street*, while standing on a giant rainbow unicorn, he will understand, because he was THERE! And for the most part my phone was off—which was HUGE and made it all the better.

Through some friends, we also discovered a super fun, non-painful baby shower. It was a "no baby shower" and I think it's a genius idea. A friend of ours got a vasectomy and his lady threw him a shower. There was sunshine, good people, booze, great food, NO KIDS, and we all pitched in to buy him a bottle of scotch and make a donation to Planned Parenthood.

Infertiles! I ask you! How many baby showers have we all had to go to, buy gifts for, and then go home and try not to cry afterwards? Folks who don't want to get married contribute to countless showers, socials, and weddings. Folks who do not plan to have children do the same. Perhaps there is something to this idea of celebrating life choices and experiences as well, no?

A very important day that has become a tradition is BED DAY. It is a day that you book off and plan to do nothing but be lazy. MAYBE walk the dog, but for the rest of the day you must relax and be a slug in bed.

Your bed is an isolated island for the day for sexy times, naps, goofing off, fort building, ordering food delivery, reading, watching movies, and keeping a cooler next to the bed filled with beer. It's magical. We have decided that it is a tradition that must continue even if we do become parents. Perhaps a hotel would be involved, but everyone needs a bed day.

Another tradition that we adore is our beloved Campiversary. Camping selfishly is amazing. Lake swimming, wet dog snuggling, hammock reading, napping, hiking, day drinking…finding a corner of your semi-private campsite to pee in because the water gets shut down and the walk to the outhouses is over twenty minutes…It's wonderful. Gross, but wonderful.

But we see the folks camping with their children and just how different it is. Carting in two-three times the amount of food and crap to set up. Taking four times as long to set up because the kids want to "help." Trying to keep them from hurting themselves or wandering off. Trying to get them to eat the meal you slaved over a fire to make when they whine that they don't WANT that for dinner anymore. Trying NOT to let them eat random flora and fauna that they find. Picking roasted marshmallow out of long hair. Breaking up fights between siblings. Attempting to institute time-outs with no discernible ways to do that. Taking them for walks or waddles because they won't stop crying. Listening to constant, and I mean CONSTANT questions. Finding ways to keep them entertained on a rainy day in a tent. Etc. etc. etc. We watch all of this happen, year after year, from our hammocks, with a drink in one hand and a book in the other. It's another one of those moments when, while being sad for our childless situation, it's hard not to be thankful for the relaxing breaks.

Later that summer we took a trip to Calgary and took a day to drive out to Lake Louise and did the Tea House hike. It was ridiculously beautiful, and despite going to the gym a lot, thinking I could handle it no problem, it was freaking TOUGH!

I've also decided that hikes are rated like spice for Thai food. This hike was rated a two out of five, and it was quite difficult. I mean, we thought it was really hard, and so did most people we passed, but then almost at the top we encountered a hiker who was eight months pregnant. There she was, just hiking and building a human, and there we were, sucking serious wind. So either it really wasn't that hard, or she's just a ridiculous superhuman or robot. But still! Two out of five! So does a four or five involve parkouring up a sheer cliff? Thai food is also often rated out of five, and I can't tell you how many times we've ordered a two or three and it's been ALL for me, because it was way too spicy for Kyle. #winning Still, in both cases of hike and delicious food: highly worth it.

After we drove back to Cowtown and showered, we went for a fabulous Boar dinner. Yup. It was awesome. I don't have much else to say about it, I just wanted to say that I ate boar cuz it sounds neat. We had fancy boar for dinner.

The main impetus for this trip was to watch two of our lovely friends out there get married. It was a beautiful wedding with spectacular scenery and so many beautiful faces. Seeing all of Kyle's old friends on the dance floor, belting out every single word to "Rock DJ," with Kyle actually dancing and having the time of his life made my heart shine. Leaving the party early because we had to get up the next morning to drive to Calgary and board a plane home was difficult, but being reminded once again that we not only have an incredible community around us in Winnipeg, but also spread all over Canada, was the battery recharge that we so sorely needed.

This vacation was a kind of renaissance of our earlier way of living life like crazy precisely BECAUSE of infertility; doing things we couldn't easily do with kids. After all, it may be our last chance to live like that for a while…but then we've been saying that for years.

Our trip was just wonderful for many reasons, but the top ones are that I got to relax for longer than a few hours, and I got to see so many beautiful friends that I love and miss. Another big reason is that I learned to let go of control over my work and clients, and trust that my incredible partner/work wife was taking excellent care of everything and everyone. I turned off my phone for a huge portion of the week, and when thoughts of work and stress started to seep back into my brain, I made a decision not to worry about it and to trust that it would be fine.

This was hard for me. I worked so hard over the years to build my business, and it was good to be so busy, but taking time away from it was difficult. Relinquishing care of my clients to someone else, even if only for a few days and to someone I trust completely, was challenging. Over the last five years I'd thrown myself into my work whenever I was hurting, and I didn't realize how much a part of me it had become.

Perhaps having no control over my ability to be a parent made me steer towards something that I could try to control a bit more. *I may not have kids, but look at how successful I can be! There's no way I could work these hours and be home with a baby!* The humbling and also freeing thing to learn was that when I came back, nothing had imploded in my absence.

Meditating on the words "I let go" has become a regular thing for me, and the more I do it, the more important it seems. Money is useless compared to mental health. I need to make space in my life, whether it's for a kid and family life, or just for art and more things that I love and miss in my life. I need to make room for things that make me feel alive and whole.

So, as SUMMER OF MO came to an end, and as I got ready for my next IVF appointment to get the ball rolling, "I let go." Or at least, I tried to let go. Fingers, toes, legs, and eyes crossed that it works, but if it didn't, we would be okay. I have a hell of a community of shoulders to cry on, and hey, camping without kids is pretty great.

IVF and COVID: Recipe for Disaster

In February of 2020, we decided to go through with IVF using donor sperm. I knew it would be a rough month, and that it would ask a lot of me, but I know some women who've gone through the process more than once, so it couldn't be THAT bad. Right?

It started innocently enough, with me taking estrogen pills orally for a week. A treat in comparison to the alternative. Having my sleep ruined, no control over my emotions (randomly cry-laughing "just because" was a regular thing) and a period that was SO VERY MUCH WORSE was the least of my worries. At least I could still work out and have the odd glass of wine! I was still in the shallow end of the pool, so to speak.

Once my period, AKA," The Bloodening" came, I had to call the clinic to let them know that I was on Day One of my cycle. Then, amid some of the worst menstrual cramps of my life, I got to go for an internal ultrasound on Day Two, which went about as well as you'd imagine. Yup, that felt great! Not messy at all! Or painful! Tra-la-la!

The double whammy was that immediately after that, I got to hand over $20k and start giving myself two to four needles in the stomach a day. Without access to wine, scotch, my workouts, or really anything that usually helps me to relax and detach. I thought surely I'd be able to keep working out. My gym routine had been a lifeline while I was taking the odd trigger shot during the IUI process and I hoped to keep it up, just pull back a bit. NOPE. My doctor said "You won't feel like it. You'll feel very heavy and sore" and I, fool that I was, scoffed. Doc then said, "Other women don't do it, and it's really not recommended after day six," and I responded with a poorly concealed "Pffft!"

"One woman rolled over in bed, and badly twisted an ovary..."

Okay. That's horrifying. Now I'm listening.

Well, he was right. I didn't feel like it. I did a couple of Yin Yoga classes (otherwise known as napping, but with instruction and fancy pillows and blankets), and once I went to the gym to walk on a treadmill. I overdid it. By *walking*.

All this to produce as many eggs as possible for retrieval and fertilization in the IVF/ICSI lab in the next few weeks. Usually, a certain number of eggs will "wake up" each month inside of a woman's ovary. One of them will be elected as their representative, and it will say to the others *I've got this, everyone! Thank you for your service. You can go now.* Then the others will commit ritual suicide. The one hero follicle will grow, like a water balloon with an egg inside of it, and once it reaches a certain size, the brain will send a signal to the ovary to ovulate/spit out the egg so it can go hang out in the uterus and wait to be fertilized while eating bonbons and watching Netflix.

Or at least this is how I picture it playing out after numerous educational/mandatory videos and interrogation sessions with our doctor. Ovaries swell a bit around ovulation, and some women (myself included) can even feel it. But they swell with even ONE follicle, and then, when that follicle gets too big, it bursts, and the egg moves to the bigger, cushier living quarters in the uterus. The daily injections were effectively turning me into a human gumball machine—getting BOTH of my ovaries to produce, farm, and grow as many follicles as possible, and to keep them in there as they grew, instead of kicking them out and turning their old room into a gym or an office or something. My ovaries were stretched WAY bigger than they'd ever been. You could see it, and you're damned right I could FEEL it. For the last week of the eleven days, I had to administer the shots, I could barely hobble around, let alone exercise. I couldn't even really stand up straight comfortably. By the time I had my final blood tests and ultrasound, and was booked for my egg retrieval procedure, I was just so glad to finally get drained/deflated/whatever it's called that I may have actually yelled "BRING IT ON!"

Part of the huge cost of IVF is the drugs. The hormones/drugs alone cost well over $5k. They also play a huge part in the disaster that is the IVF process. Because it all depends on how you're developing day to day, with meds that are ridiculously expensive, you only get a few days' worth at a time. So my mom and I went to the clinic, waited in line, got my blood tests and ultrasounds, then got a prescription to take to the pharmacy that deals with the clinic.

We drove down and handed in the prescription, then waited some more, then the pharmacist took us into a private room to explain how to mix, assemble, and administer the shots. I feel like they should have a smartboard for this, because despite having the typed out "how to" paper provided for the shots and nodding my head along to all of the demonstrations, my palms were sweaty and the voice in my head shrieking "I AM NOT A NURSE, BUDDY! NOR AM I A GENIUS CHEMIST! I AM NOT QUALIFIED FOR THIS IN THE SLIGHTEST!" was so loud that I only absorbed so much instruction. I had already had some experience with giving myself trigger shots during our IUI attempts the previous year, but this was so much more confusing. My mom was with me, and she looked positively shell-shocked to see what I was going to have to do.

That night I only had to administer two shots, one of which was in a preloaded pen, so all I had to do was set the right dosage, attach the needle tip, pinch some flesh two inches away from my belly button (but not above it), clean the skin, stab myself and push the plunger all the way down. The second shot was much more complicated. I had to take the safety cap off of the syringe, put a Q-cap on (which I did backwards the first time), attach it to vial #1 with liquid in it, suck up a certain amount of liquid, take vial #1 off, attach vial #2, add the liquid, swirl (don't shake!), suck the mixture up into the syringe, take off vial #2, attach vial #3, repeat what I did with vial #2, snap off the q-cap, put on the needle tip, remove the safety, make sure there were no air bubbles, wipe the skin, pinch some flesh, stab myself and push the plunger. Easy peasy, right?

I did not miss my calling when I didn't become a nurse. In fact, I felt more like a combination of The Swedish Chef, Beaker, and Heisenberg when I was trying to do all of this, but while also sobbing because I felt so overwhelmed and stupid because the pharmacist had walked me through this only that morning!

At any rate, I did the thing, had my little cry, wiped my face and nose, and called the other real estate agent I had been trying to negotiate with before the clock struck needle-o'clock to resume our work/argument. Yeah, that went about as well as can be expected. Fun times.

The following eleven days involved about forty to fifty shots in the belly, with tests, ultrasounds, and new and exciting types of hormones being added to the mix, which, of course, all had their own method for mixing and administration. The shots, side effects, and ALL of the hormones were making me miserable. I was sore and exhausted. I was also still working because I was self-employed and couldn't afford to pay someone else to take care of my clients for me, plus I knew I'd have to take three days off after the retrieval. Showing houses while bent over was sort of my jam for those weeks. It didn't get easier, but I got more used to it. The side effects of pain when I walked, drove over a bump, jostled, or twisted got worse as the time went on as well, so that was exciting. But all I really wanted, pretty much all of the time, was cake. I love baked goods anyway, but my cake cravings were much more insistent than usual.

By the end of it, Kyle and I had a system. At 8:50 p.m. every night, I'd go and start laying everything out on the bathroom counter to get ready on time. Kyle would pull up a chair in the hallway outside the bathroom and sit there with the dog to be my moral support. He would pull up spa music, nature sounds, or *Harry Potter* music (shut up, it brings me joy) on his phone to help calm me while I worked. Then he brought me cake. And daisies, because they make me smile. He felt so helpless, having to watch me go through all of this for us, so he really picked up the slack to be as helpful to me as he could, and kept me in cake and daisies and many hugs. I think I'll keep him.

I had a bruise pattern like a smiley face around my belly button, but I assure you that I did NOT feel smiley. Finding any unused, unbruised, un-ouchy skin on my swollen belly for injection sites was proving difficult, but afterward there was cake, so…balance.

IVF SURVIVAL KIT:
1. Money (think stacks of gold coins, like Scrooge McDuck)
2. Outfits that don't involve pants or tight things
3. Cozy blankets
4. Go-to movies or shows that bring comfort
5. Things that make you smile (i.e., daisies)
6. Cake

In the midst of all of this, I had a day from hell. I set the alarm and got up early to dutifully go and wait in line outside of the building at the clinic for the umpteenth time, for my early "appointment." All ten of us waiting in line always had the same appointment time. So we waited outside, eyeing each other up and giving weak smiles. It was a Saturday, so a nurse from the clinic upstairs had to come down to let us into the building, where we waited in line again to sign into the building, then waited in line for our "turn" up the elevator, and then in another line to sign in for our actual appointment at the front desk of the clinic. While we were being let into the building, a dude literally stepped in front of me and elbowed me in the face to block me from getting into the building before his wife. I was so dazed that by the time I got all of the lining up and signing in done, I was last. I then had the joy of sitting in the waiting room, helplessly watching it empty out while every other person went ahead of me. I was hungry and I had to pee and I was hormonal and exhausted, and this was all helping *immensely* with my mood.

When the nurse finally came to get me, I didn't even know what time it was. I went into the examination room, disrobed, and got up into the stirrups to wait for whatever doctor was doing the ultrasounds that day. About twenty-five minutes later, in he came. We did the ultrasound, and he told me I needed to go back to the pharmacy for another three days or so of shots, then get some extra shots to get me good and ready for the egg retrieval procedure next weekend sometime. I was stoked to hear that there was an end in sight to this part of the process, but then he said I needed to go for some more blood tests, and since it was a weekend, the clinic's blood person wasn't on duty, so I'd have to go to one of two labs that was open to give blood. In the whole city. At 9:30 a.m. on a Saturday, he was sending me to one of the busiest walk-ins around.

I pulled out my cellphone to cancel on some clients I was supposed to connect with that afternoon and headed over to the clinic with the lab to get my bloods done. I walked in the back door of the building, into the long hallway that curves around to the lab and waiting rooms, but after about two steps I came to a stop. Because that WAS the line. It was standing room only, in a building packed like an overstuffed sardine can, with a two-and-a-half-hour wait. I wished so much that I'd brought a book with me, or water, or snacks, or a camping chair, but then I would've had to carry all of that crap as well as my winter parka—'cause Canada in February. I called Kyle to whine that the day was shot and tried not to burst into hysterical tears while I stood and waited.

SECONDARY LIST/WAITING ROOM SURVIVAL KIT:
1. water, for the love of God
2. snacks
3. books, games, or other distractions,
4. phone charger, if your book or games are on your phone

5. the will to live
6. coffee (which tends to help with the will to live)
* during Covid-19, you may not be able to consume water or snacks anyway, what with the mask and all.

While I was waiting, my phone rang. It was my mom. "I wanted to let you know that Gran is in the hospital, so you should try to get down here today, if you can." My stomach, which was just starting to unwind, twisted further.

When I was FINALLY finished giving blood samples, I fought my way through the lineup to get out of the building and headed to the pharmacy, which was only about a ten-minute drive away, and conveniently right next to the hospital where my family was anxiously gathered around my grandmother.

I handed over another buttload of money to the pharmacist and got more instructions on the new addition to the family of syringes to assemble, IKEA-style, but without the cute names with umlauts. I grabbed a snack and some water, tossed the meds in the car, and headed to the hospital.

When I found my way to my grandmother's bedside, I was struck by how frail she looked. She'd always been a trim lady, but she'd been shrinking over the last few years. Still smart as a whip and stubborn as an old Scottish Granny—which I guess she was—she still lived on her own in an apartment, albeit with lots of help from my mom and aunts. Before she went into the hospital, she'd had a fall and was all bruised up, then she'd had another fall while in hospital. She was so badly bruised everywhere that I was afraid to touch her. She had sustained a head injury and was more out of consciousness than in, but we held her hand and talked into her ear to let her know that we were there.

I am thankful that I was able to be there, because within an hour of my arrival, with all of us gathered around her, Grandma took her last breaths. She lived a long and full life, and that's just the way human existence works, but it's still sad to say goodbye to someone who has been a constant in your life since day one. Then I quickly and rudely had to excuse myself from the bedside vigil and hug/cryfest to make a phone call. As I stood there weeping with my family, it had suddenly occurred to me that it was February. In Winnipeg, Canada. And I had just left about $1,500 worth of liquid vials of medication and syringes in my car...to freeze. Did I just ruin it?! Fuuuuuuuuuuck fuckity fuck FUCK.

I ran down the hall and called the pharmacy to ask them what they thought of my situation. The pharmacist said that it was probably fine, but just barely, and that I should really get home and get the meds into the house to acclimatize to room temperature. Oh, thank God. Well, crisis averted, but it still felt awful to have to basically say goodbye to my family and JUST deceased grandmother. Of course they understood, but I still felt gross and cried all the way home, where Kyle was waiting for me with literal open arms and chocolate to offer me.

So, one "day from hell" down, but with the good fortune to be able to be with my family and grandmother for an important afternoon. If I could survive a crap day like that, in the midst of IVF treatments, surely I could survive the rest.

Retrieval

Despite wanting the pain and treatments to stop and wanting so badly to be drained of all of the swelling and excess fluid, I was fucking terrified of the egg retrieval. I got that if we were successful there, I would get to experience the "miracle" of childbirth—which would be infinitely worse. That is also terrifying. And at least if you go through that hell, you usually get a baby at the end of it! I mean, I can't be the only one who has shared wide-eyed looks with friends as they announce their pregnancy like *You are gonna go through some shit, lady...but CONGRATULATIONS!*

I'd been warned that the retrieval would not be fun. At all. But apparently the drugs were going to be interesting, so that was a new experience to look forward to. Kyle and I rolled up to the clinic the full two hours before our appointment time, as instructed. I had not had anything to eat or drink since the evening before, also as instructed, and given the drugs and looming procedure, that makes sense and all, but I am not a morning person. I am especially not a morning person when I cannot have breakfast, or coffee, or even water. I did bring my book, though, in an attempt to keep my mind busy.

We sat in the waiting room for a few moments, and then a nurse came and attempted to call my name. She missed the mark entirely, but I knew what she was trying to say, so off we went! She led us down to the opposite "wing" of the clinic from every other appointment I'd ever had through the years. I'd seen women go down this hallway before but didn't know where they were headed. Now that I was walking in that direction, I realized that this wing was for the more invasive procedures—like egg retrievals. It occurred to me that none of the women I'd seen walk down this hallway looked like they were wobbling on shaky legs, while obviously nervous as hell. Maybe they just hid it better than me. Or maybe to the others in the waiting room, I too looked calm and collected, and not at all like I might poop my pants at any moment.

The nurse led us around a corner and into a room with three recliners with three regular chairs next to them, all separated with tracks on the ceiling for curtains. She then gave me something to help me relax that tasted like chalk and went under my tongue. I settled into the pajamas they provided and the Lazyboy—directly between two other couples, separated only with curtains. So... SUPER private... but it was nice to hear the women beside me relaying their stories of being miserable without being able to exercise (not just me!), or the other one whose husband told the nurse how she fainted the first time he administered the needles to her tummy. Kyle looked at me, squeezed my hand, and whispered "Thank you for not making me do that to you." I read my book and slowly felt slightly fuzzy from the chalk-thingie in my parched mouth. The nurse came back, and it was my turn for an IV. It was uncomfortable, but I was thankful that it wasn't in my hand because that has always grossed me right out, AND she gave me a large sperm-shaped stress ball to squeeze while she inserted the IV into my arm, which provided endless giggles for Kyle and I. They would not let us take it home.

But then I started to worry about pooping. These morning appointments usually mess with my morning routine—including my body's normal routine, ahem, and I started to wonder what the best course of action would be. I mean, I WAS just about to have someone all up in my grill, and I didn't need the added discomfort of not being able to go to the washroom before the torture began. The nurse told me to waddle down to the bathroom, IV in tow, one last time before my procedure anyway, so, problem solved. I'm not telling you this to gross you out, but because in my mind it's funny that THAT was something that was suddenly extremely concerning to me in the midst of all of this. Also, consider it a precursor for reading the parts about the procedure itself. If a poop mention is too much for you, you might want to skip ahead to the post-procedure part of this chapter.

When I got settled in my chair again and discovered that I was a bit too fuzzy-headed to read, we just tried to chill and wait for my turn in the stirrups. We tried to stay calm as we heard the woman on my right get taken to the procedure room, which was right next to us with only a very thin wall dividing the space. Yeah, it's REALLY difficult to remain calm when you're already really nervous, and then you get to hear the woman before you SCREAMING DURING HER PROCEDURE. Yup, SUPER encouraging. The lady to my left and I laughed nervously, saying through the curtain "Well…I don't like the sound of THAT." When the nurse came back and said "Okay Morwenna, it's time. Let's get you up," I stared at her, wide-eyed, and said that the theatrics of the woman before me had just made me incredibly nervous. The nurse said it was all good, and that I'd feel some pressure. You've gotta love how medical professionals say things like "pressure" but mean "PAIN." Pressure, discomfort. Bullshit. Just say *This will be painful, but it won't last long.* I'm not sure if that would've helped, but at least it would've been the truth.

I had spent the previous few weeks turning my ovaries into a follicle farm. I had ten follicles that had matured and swollen until my ovaries were WAY bigger than normal. These follicles are like water balloons that will hopefully have, somewhere inside them, a microscopic egg. At our last appointment with our doctor, I had a sudden brainwave and had asked him: "Wait. You need to do an egg retrieval…but the eggs will not have ovulated or moved to my uterus yet? So… how will you be retrieving them, if not through the …er…direct route?" I sort of regret asking that question, because he then informed me that they'd have to go up through my vagina and puncture each follicle to drain them individually through the walls of my vagina and ovaries on the other side. When I asked how they'd know where to…dig…he said they'd use the internal ultrasound machine, with a needle and catheter attached. I pictured a bayonet. Why? I don't know. Because that's how my brain works sometimes.

So yes, the procedure was extremely unpleasant, but I was determined not to scream like the first lady and scare the hell out of the woman going after me. As they settled my legs and feet into the stirrups and calf-troughs (technical term?) the nurse asked me how many glasses of wine *until I'm done.* I didn't understand the question. I said, "I dunno…one or two?"

I didn't realize that she meant *how many glasses of wine to get you plastered.* I choose to stop drinking after one or two, but don't feel inebriated much—is it too late to change my answer?! Please give me lots of drugs! I DO NOT WANT TO FEEL THIS!

Well, she gave me a couple glasses of wine's worth of Fentanyl. So now that's a thing that I've tried. Honestly, I didn't feel inebriated, and still felt much, much pain from the stabby bayonet draining. At one point, the doctor between my knees said, "You need to relax. Stop tensing." I wanted to make some snarky comment about him being able to relax while having his balls stabbed and drained repeatedly, but through the wall of a different organ and had a momentary glimpse into why the woman before me was probably yelling. Instead, I squeezed Kyle's hand and we launched into singing a rousing rendition of "Eye of The Tiger" to get me through it. So the woman after me didn't hear screaming through the wall, but she may have heard Kyle and I singing out of tune. I hope it gave her comfort, or at least a "WTF" moment.

After the procedure and a little recovery "nap" back in the recliner, they handed Kyle a prescription for...something...and sent us on our way to the pharmacy. They also told me to eat salty things, because my body had gotten used to having excess fluid in my abdomen for a few weeks, even though it was abnormal and didn't belong there. Apparently, once the fluid is drained, your body can panic, wondering who stole all of the fluid, and it will start trying to replace it. That fluid can work its way up to your lungs and be incredibly dangerous. Well, if that's not completely terrifying, and an awesome excuse to stop at McDonald's on the way to the pharmacy, I don't know what is!

When we got home from the pharmacy, I went to lie down, while saying to Kyle, "I don't know what the big deal is with Fentanyl, I feel nothing. I don't even feel tir..." And then I blacked out and lost four and a half hours. When I woke up, I happily moved to the living room recliner, settled in, and watched movies while eating salty things and assuring my mom and friends that I was fine. Sore, but fine. In the end, my ten follicles produced six eggs. Not too shabby! Now we would have to wait for updated info every couple of days, telling us how many eggs were successfully fertilized into embryos, and then how many made it to day five, the blastocyst stage.

I took the required three days off of work as I wasn't supposed to move much at all, and it wasn't hard as I was still quite sore and didn't FEEL like doing anything. I was once again reminded how amazing my village of people is when my mom and a few friends all came by to drop off food for us so that we wouldn't have to cook. Not too shabby at all. A week after the procedure, I had my last phone call with the nurses at the clinic, who informed me that five embryos had made it to "blast stage." Five! Five is HUGE. I've had friends go through IVF and end up with only one or two, or in some cases NONE. This was absolutely fabulous news, so I called my people to jump up and down, and Kyle and I had some champagne that night to celebrate. They just had to send our five embryos for genetic testing, (which does cost an extra $4k or so but can vastly increase chances of success) to determine how many of them were healthy, viable, and wouldn't miscarry. I asked the nurse if expecting two or three in the end was reasonable, and she said absolutely.

Nightgowns and French Fries

A while after dad died, mom and I were home late one night, when she suddenly realized that the movie that we had rented from Blockbuster was about to be overdue. Being the rule-follower that she is, Mom decided to hop in the car and go drop off the movie really quick, before it was too late. She tucked her nightgown into some sweats and took off.

About twenty minutes later, she came bursting through the door wide-eyed, cry-laughing, hair dishevelled, nightgown hanging down one side where it had come untucked, looking frantically for her purse while clutching a carton of French fries. When I asked her what the hell had happened, she told me that, on the way back from dropping the movie, she had passed by a McDonald's and suddenly wanted some fries. So she pulled through the drive-thru only to find that she had forgotten her wallet at home. The teenager working the window smirked at her profuse apologies and promises to come right back, and simply handed her the fries and told her not to worry about it. She was MORTIFIED and determined to go right back and pay the boy. I couldn't stop laughing.

Well, she did it. She drove back, went through the drive-thru again, without actually ordering anything, but now it was a different person in the window. She explained what had happened and handed over the change to pay for the purloined fries and drove home. When I pointed out that the kid who had given her the fries in the first place was now most likely in trouble for doing so BECAUSE SHE WENT BACK, she was crestfallen, until I took her picture because I needed to remember the image and she joined me in bursting into uncontrollable laughter. This, ladies, and gentlemen, is where my need for order and rules comes from. It also explains why I don't own a nightgown—I don't want to increase my chances of accidentally wearing it out in public.

My mom grew up in the '50s and '60s and was a self-proclaimed "goody two-shoes." Her whole family was (and is) heavily involved with the Presbyterian church and Scottish country dancing events, and she was also advanced a year in school. So she was a young smarty-pants-goody-two-shoes-twinkle-toes. She was teaching in a classroom by the time she was nineteen—and then met my dad at a Scottish Country Dance social.

They dated, fell in love, were married, had my brother and I, and lived happily together for over two decades until Dad's death. My parents lived and loved each other and grew together for twenty-two years until Dad was suddenly gone—mom had spent more time in her life with my dad than without him. And then, in the blink of an eye, she was on her own—a single mother to two bitchy and hurting teenagers. We cried together, when I wasn't pushing her away, and then she picked herself up, dusted herself off, and went into business mode: back to work, back to cooking and cleaning and paying the bills, and trying to be both parents to a fourteen-year-old basket case with a brand new chip on her shoulder, and an almost nineteen-year-old man who was determined to move to Alberta as soon as he could.

Depression runs in our family, and both my mom and I have struggled with it forever, but she got out of bed every damn day and carried on. When I point this out to her as an example of how strong she is, she shrugs it off and simply says "Well, I had to." My mom is fucking formidable, and anyone who doesn't agree can fight me. The world pulled the rug out from under her, and she rallied. I want my kid to know her.

Around the time that Dad died, a married couple that my folks had been close with split up. Dad's best friend, Jay, was suddenly a single parent of two, AND he had just lost his best friend. Mom and Jay started to hang out to support one another through this shitshow of a year. Naturally, they fell in love, and decided to move in together—and now they had four angry kids to deal with.

It took several years, but Jay waited ever so patiently for me to grow up and realize how great he is. He doesn't need to replace my dad; he is his own wonderful creature. My dad was an incredible man, and I love and miss him every day of my life. Jay is a different incredible man who can't possibly ever know or understand just how much he has shaped who I am.

All three of my parents are amazing and have given me so much to be proud of and aspire to. One of the reasons I want a family so badly is because I want my kids to know their grandparents.

Part
7

Waiting

While we waited anxiously for two weeks until the test results were in, and for our next meeting with our doctor, Covid-19 found its way to Canada. As things made their way into a lockdown/isolation situation, we were informed that our next meeting with our doctor would be over the phone. I was actually relieved to hear that as that clinic was always so jam-packed with people. Kyle and I hovered over his phone, on speaker, as our doctor informed us that only one embryo had made it through genetic testing. One viable embryo. One last shot at a family, after almost seven years of trying all of the things. I felt like I'd been slapped. I asked him if it was because of my age, and he hesitated, and then said, "Yes. Most likely."

I burst into tears and tried to keep it together to ask what the next steps were. To give our one last shot the best chance of success, I would need to go through another month of testing and monitoring. I'd have to take three different hormones and go for many, many early-morning fevered-Beatles-fan-style-frenzied appointments for blood tests, ultrasounds, and a uterine biopsy to determine the exact dosage of drugs to put me on and the exact hour in my cycle that my body would be most "receptive" and likely to accept and implant the embryo. Then, at that same time next cycle, we'd do the embryo transfer and hope for me to get knocked up. Well, that wasn't ideal, but of course I'd do it. Let's go!

Oh, wait…we couldn't. The clinic was closed indefinitely until it was deemed safe to reopen after Covid-19 wasn't so much of a threat anymore. *Well, how long will that be?* No clue. *Will you contact us to tell us when it's time and you're open again?* No. I was just going to have to stalk their websites daily to figure that out for myself. Fan-fucking-tastic. *Oh, and try to relax, Morwenna.* No problem.

Of course the clinic had to be closed to keep everyone safe from the coronavirus. The way we were always packed in there like sheep or a Black Friday lineup on a first come, first served basis for our tests. The amount of lab tests required for all of us that could be spent on Covid testing—closing made sense. I knew this.

But knowing why didn't make the waiting any easier. The two-and-a-half months we spent in self-isolation were stressful, to say the least. I kept wondering how long it would take to reopen, and if when we finally did do the transfer, it wouldn't take simply because of my age. I later found out that the age a woman is when the eggs are retrieved is more important than how old she is at the time of transfer, but at this time I was unaware of that fact. I had regrets, thinking that if I'd just done things in *January* instead of *February*, maybe I'd be pregnant right then. I knew that it was "only a few more months," but it had been "just a few more months" for SO LONG, and in my quarantine-addled brain (and lack of hair dye or usual grooming) I looked in the mirror and saw rapid aging, like that scene at the end of *Indiana Jones and the Last Crusade*.

Kyle and I swung wildly back and forth from being terrified it wouldn't work, to being terrified that it *would* work, and everything that would bring. Being so close, and having our last chance locked in a freezer somewhere was rough, to say the least.

Eventually, the clinic did partially reopen. They'd communicate with me through an app I had to download, and I'd have to go to all of my appointments with proper PPE, and alone. My ERA (uterine biopsy in the middle of the "trial month" with all the hormones) procedure sucked to do alone. It literally only lasted for five seconds, but it was painful and would've been nice to have a Kyle with me to hold my hand. Though I'm not sure which hurt more—the procedure itself, or the $1100 bill they handed me afterwards for a procedure that we had thought was already covered by all of the other fees. Nope! I handed over my credit card yet again. I *was* suddenly super grateful that I didn't have to do the egg retrieval alone in a Covid-19 world. The woman before me had screamed, and I'd needed Kyle there to hold my hand and stroke my face and sing a montage song with me to get through it. I cannot imagine how hard it is for all of those strong women undergoing that awful procedure, so exposed and vulnerable, with only a doctor and a couple of nurses in the room with them. I also got to go off of most of the hormones soon after that, to await my final "bloodening" to start the next cycle for real. Next month would be the actual show, after this messy dress rehearsal.

About a week later, we started the official FET (frozen embryo transfer) cycle. I started back on all of the wicked fun meds, went back for multiple tests and ultrasound, and we booked the date for the transfer. As luck would have it, a wonderful colleague looked after my clients yet again so that Kyle, Charlie the dog, and I could go camping for three days to relax before the big day. It was absolutely lovely—I swam constantly, we read books and napped and drank in our hammocks, and I more or less had my phone OFF for three glorious days. Then, we drove back to the city, showered, and I worked a couple of days to tie up some more loose ends and make sure all was well with my clients, before taking another two days off for the procedure. I had my last glass of wine and attempted to get a good night's sleep before getting up to go and stand in line once again to hopefully get knocked up.

The transfer was relatively uneventful except for the whole "having a life changing medical procedure during a global pandemic" thing. Oh, and my poor, poor bladder. And of course Kyle still hadn't been able to come with me for any procedures in the last couple of months. We still waited like herded sheep, but more orderly sheep, spaced out, with masks on. They told me to come with a full bladder because apparently it helps to make the uterus lie flat.

It's important to note that my bladder is the size of a walnut at the best of times. I drink a lot of water and have never taken my mother's old advice of "always pee before leaving the house" for granted. I'm delightful on a road trip. Anyway, my appointment was at 10:30 a.m. and I was to be there a bit early. So I got there at about 10:15 a.m. With a full bladder. By 11 a.m., I was entertaining everyone in line with my pee-pee dance while standing on my socially distanced piece of tape on the floor.

At 11:04 they finally came and let me in, but I wasn't allowed to pee before the procedure unless I would be able to pee for about three seconds and then somehow magically turn it off, leaving my bladder still mostly full. Uh... no. That wasn't going to be possible. So, I changed into the gown and extremely fetching hair and foot booties, screwed what I hoped wasn't a horribly bitchy expression onto my face, and in I went.

As they bustled around, prepping things and putting my legs back into those stirrup/calf trough things again, they handed me a picture of the blastocyst embryo and I almost burst into hormone-and-urine-addled tears. *This is why I'm here*, I thought. *It's you and me, kid. Let's try not to let each other down.* One nurse did an ultrasound on my tummy—and while it was a welcome change not to have an internal ultrasound for once, she pressed down right on my full bladder—while the doc did his work from under my hood, so to speak. A bonus was that it was actually my own doctor this time, and he's lovely. Getting your own doctor at this place feels about as rare as a Bigfoot sighting, so this was pretty great. He pointed to a spot on the ultrasound screen and announced that that was the "target" we were aiming for with the catheter to deposit the embryo, and said, "That's the comfiest spot for baby to make a home."

After that, we hung out and chatted, awkwardly ignoring the fact that I was still spread eagle on the table with my legs in those holder thingies, while we waited for a nurse to take the catheter back into the lab to check and make sure that he had, in fact, deposited the embryo inside of me. Those things are microscopic, so the only way to know it had been successfully transferred was to check the empty catheter to make sure that the embryo wasn't still stuck inside it somewhere. He said that if it was, we would simply try again, and we'd know that the embryo was probably female, because she was being stubborn! I chuckled and shook a finger at him, but given how stubborn I know myself to be …he might have had a point.

In the end, it wasn't the worst procedure I've experienced, but no day at the beach. I think the added emotionally charged situation of THIS IS YOUR LAST CHANCE. PERIOD. made it more difficult. I swear I heard RuPaul's voice telling me *Don't fuck it up*. I do feel that I deserve a gold star for not peeing all over my doctor and the table, and I didn't cry much, so yay, me! As I got dressed, had what may be the most glorious pee of my life, and went back through the waiting room and hallway to leave, I passed the other women still waiting in a socially distanced line. One of them also had a transfer appointment for 10:30, and also very much had to pee. It was now well after 11:30. Godspeed, lady. I am so sorry but also not sorry that they let me in first.

The next fun part was learning about the super restricted diet I needed to be on, plus removing coffee—even decaf—and exercise from my life for a couple of weeks. That morning, I had made myself a full French press of half-caff coffee. This makes two cups of coffee, so I had had one and left the other for myself as a treat when I got home from the procedure. Finding out that I wasn't going to be able to have even decaf for a few weeks made me miserable. I went home to rest and made Kyle pour out my remaining coffee because I couldn't bring myself to do it. I saluted and sang Taps while he did it. It was a somber occasion.

Kyle went grocery shopping for the delicious birdseed, veggie, seafood, and health food diet I was about to get serious about, and I tried to stay away from work. But the thing is, this business doesn't give you a minute, even if you plan for it and have wonderful people covering for you. In this business, work happens when it happens. Sometimes I might randomly get a day or two off and it's grand. Sometimes I simply have to put my head down and work ridiculously long hours for weeks or months at a time. I did my best for a couple of days, but avoiding stress just plain wasn't possible for me right then. Would this be the reason it wouldn't work? My LAST CHANCE at a family, ruined because I couldn't slow down properly? What if I cheated and had a cookie? Was that bad for the embryo? (The answer is no, I've spoken to many experts and read multiple articles, but my busy, hormone-soaked brain still worried). But then spoke to some friends I know who are also going through the process, and only one of them was doing the restricted diet. One of the ones who wasn't had the same doctor as me, too! So, perhaps I could calm down a bit on the fascist diet situation. Breathe, Trevenen.

Kyle

Learning you can't have biological children is not a good time. It's hard to learn you'll never have a child that shares your blood. It's a bad day when you learn that. And yet, life had prepared me for this moment. Being adopted myself taught me that blood isn't what makes a family. What makes a family is people who care about each other, who show love to each other, who learn from each other. My parents taught me that. It has helped me come to terms with my microdeletion of the Y chromosome. All this sucks, but I'm doing okay. Honestly. Compared to Mo, I've got it easy.

Mo is strong. And we are both finding strength in making the decision to stop trying and move forward. What I mean is that this is it. This is our last attempt at trying to have a child. Regardless of the outcome, we will know within a year what our path shall be. This cycle of our hopes rising and falling will finally be over, and (whatever may happen) we can finally move forward together. My warrior queen and I.

The End of the Road

I'm terrified it won't work. I'm terrified it will work. And I'm trying not to stress out, all the while pumping myself full of hormones that make reasonable thinking damn near impossible, three times a bloody day. I am a walking pharmacy. These pills slow down my immune system to prevent my body from rejecting the embryo. (Yes, you read that right. I'm suppressing my immune system. In a global pandemic). These other ones thicken my uterine lining and make me nauseous, weepy, angry, desperately sad and anxious, and mess with my sleep and strength. I call those ones the Dumbledore pills, because of that scene in *Harry Potter and the Half-Blood Prince* where Harry and Dumbledore are hunting horcruxes in a cave, and Harry has to keep feeding water that is hurting Dumbledore down his throat, despite him crying and begging for it to stop. It was for the greater good.

I am also on other pills to prevent infection, and a whole lot of hormones that are vaguely believed to be helpful in these situations: some that are suppositories with other great side effects, so that's fun; and some that are administered with a needle, but in the butt this time, so that's fun for the whole family because I can't get the angle right, so Kyle has to help me (see: improvised and unsupervised couples therapy, or working through aggression in relationships). I get irrational and emotional and nauseous; Kyle gets to stab me every three days. It's a win-win.

If it works, I will finally get the title of "Mom," which is all I've wanted for so much of my life. I will get to watch Kyle be an incredible father, and share moments shaping (and hopefully not fucking up) this tiny human to be a positive influence on the world. Christmas won't be painful anymore, because I will get to watch the magic of Christmas in

their eyes. I will take them camping, and hold them when they cry, and share in their joys and laughter. My house will be a disaster, and I'll have to learn to live with it. I'll get to experience a love like no other. Kyle and I will finally get to be in "the club" with our friends who had kids and slowly faded away, both from being busy, and from it being too painful for us to be around them much. It will be amazing, and wonderful, and a blessing, and terrifying, and harder than anything I'm sure I've ever done. And I can't fucking wait.

If it doesn't work out for us with this last try, I will shut myself up into a dark room for a month to mourn and drink and otherwise deal with my despair in a less-than-healthy way. But then I will pick myself up, dust myself off, and LIVE my damn life. Kyle and I are of course petrified that it won't work, but we comfort ourselves with all of the phenomenal things that we will be able to do with our lives, possibly BECAUSE we won't have children—time and money-suckers as they are.

Our life will always have a hole in it, for the life we had wanted and didn't get to have, but you can be damned sure that we will live it to the fullest—simply because we can. Does this mean it *wasn't* worth it? All of those years of pain, money, and emotional and physical trauma for nothing? I refuse to accept that.

The fork in the path before me leads to two very different lives, but both will be rewarding, beautiful and painful in their own way. This journey has been brutal, isolating, heart-wrenching, tragic, sadly/oddly funny, and character-shaping. It has taught me a tonne, tried and strengthened my marriage, and made me into who I am. I like who I've become, sharp edges and all, and I'm proud of how much I've grown and learned. Building character is fucking exhausting, but people who lack character are boring.

So take heart, dear infertiles—we are so much more than this. We will get through this, no matter what the outcome, and *none* of it was a waste.